T0199160

I Died
but Lived
to Tell My Story

RONALD W. PAGE

WESTBOW
PRESS®
A DIVISION OF THOMAS NELSON
& ZONDERVAN

WestBow Press books may be ordered through booksellers or by contacting:

WestBow Press
A Division of Thomas Nelson & Zondervan
1663 Liberty Drive
Bloomington, IN 47403
www.westbowpress.com
1 (866) 928-1240

ISBN: 978-1-5127-2230-7 (sc)
ISBN: 978-1-5127-2231-4 (hc)
ISBN: 978-1-5127-2229-1 (e)

Library of Congress Control Number: 2015919951

Print information available on the last page.

WestBow Press rev. date: 12/01/2015

Contents

CHAPTER 1

My Humble Beginnings

My growing up years gave me much pleasure. That was before I knew how my life would change. I am Ronald Page and was born on August 9, 1955. I am the son of James R. (Jim) Page Sr. and Joan Smith Page and the little brother of James R. (Rick) Page Jr. I grew up in a small mill village located in the town of Clinton, South Carolina, which had a population of about 10,000 people.

My mom and dad both worked at the local cotton mill, just as most people who lived in a mill village in those days did. Everyone seemed to live their lives in the same ways. People didn't know they were from humble beginnings, because everyone appeared to have the same things and lived in the same environment.

Many good people and friends came from the mill village—some of the best people I have ever met. Most employees at the local mill company bought their power and water from the company and shopped at the local mill store. The mill store had everything a family needed: meats, vegetables, groceries, dry goods, appliances, and furniture. It even had paint for painting houses, along with other hardware items. As for automobiles (if someone was blessed enough to afford one), people bought their gas and tires at the filling station—also owned by the mill company. It was a routine way of life that most became accustomed to. Some mill folks thought they couldn't survive without the mill store. All the houses and folks around us looked the same, making life simple. That's what we thought at that time. Everyone knew their neighbors, milkmen, mail carriers, trash men, and so forth.

Life was hard, even back then, but as kids—not baby goats—we were not aware of doing without things that others had. Well, that was grownup stuff. We didn't know about lack of money, bills, house payments, or the ability to pay for those things. We didn't even know that some folks outside the village had air conditioning! Air conditioning was what the big stores uptown used to keep the inside of their stores cool for shoppers. The coldest place I can remember—when I did get a chance to go—was the Broadway Theater on Broad Street in downtown Clinton. Air conditioning—what in the world was that?

As kids, there were many nights when my brother and I would sleep on the floor or do what was called camping out. Camping out meant we would sleep in the backyard—also known as the back alley. Usually, there were several friends involved when we camped out. (Today, kids call it a sleepover. It just wasn't correct for *mill-hillians* to call it a sleepover, because we were rowdy.)

I can remember sleeping on the floor in the summertime, with both the front and back doors wide open. The open doors allowed us to catch a cool breeze so that we could fall asleep. If it hadn't been for the large oak trees shading most houses, folks would have been in big trouble with the heat during the daytime. I'd like to thank the late Mr. P.S. Bailey for having the foresight to plant those oak trees back in the 1800s.

In those days, most of the mill houses had outhouses, which they used up until the 1950s when the mill company started putting toilets inside the houses. Most of them were enclosed on the back porches. During the summer, we would also go to the local swimming pool, which, yes—you guessed it—was owned by the mill company. If we didn't have the fifteen cents admission cost for the pool, we just got under the hosepipe at home. The best times were when it rained, and we got to play in it—unless there was thunder and lightning. One of the best things we had back then was our homemade slip-and-slide. It was made by taking someone's old, discarded vinyl rug and placing it on the ground in the back alley. We would wet it, put dishwashing detergent on it to make it slippery, and slide on it for hours. Lord, help our backsides if we hit a dry spot on that vinyl rug!

My friends, my brother, and I didn't know it, but we also invented skateboards (not like the ones today). We would borrow our dads' tools, take our skates apart, and nail them on to a short plank of wood. We spent many hours on those skateboards and incurred many injuries. Man, we kept the nurse at the mill clinic, Ms. Nell, busy with all the injuries we received from our homemade projects. Yep, if your parents worked at the mill and you got a scrape or small cut, the mill nurse would fix you right up at no charge.

I can see where today's kids are spoiled and don't experience the excitement of Christmas the way we did. Kids today seem to get toys and things every other week. It seems parents are buying presents and stuff during the year just to pacify kids. We played games such as marbles, back-alley football, and fox and dogs, and we used a cardboard box to slide down grassy hills for fun. We also made our own wooden wagons in which to push each other around. Today, kids get go-carts, four-wheelers, motorbikes, cell phones, video games, and even cars if they are old enough.

Don't take all that out of context if today's parents can afford those things. But I think it detracts from the real meaning of Christmas and puts some families in a position of financial hardship because they want to keep up with the Joneses. I too was guilty of some of these things when I became a parent. First Timothy 6:10 King James Version (KJV) says, "For the love of money is the root of all evil: which while some coveted after, they have erred from the faith, and pierced themselves through many sorrows."

Christmas today seems to begin right after the Fourth of July holiday. Times have changed because when I was growing up, Christmas holidays began the day after Thanksgiving. I think it has a lot to do with living fast and satisfying commercial greed nowadays. Years in the mill village seemed a bit slower, and people weren't in such a hurry. Stores were closed on Sunday. Folks visited kin, went to church, and had Sunday dinner. Eating a lot of fried chicken on Sunday afternoons was the norm, and boy, was it good! During my childhood, the grownups ate first, and then the kids ate. In today's world, kids eat first. If you sit down to eat and a child doesn't like what's on the table, the parents jump up and run to McDonald's for the child. If we had told our dads or moms that we didn't want or like what was on the table, they would have jumped up all right. They would've jumped up and torn up our hind ends. Disrespecting parents was not tolerated.

It wasn't until I was grown that I realized a chicken had more than just wings and legs. I think we all need to slow down and focus on the most important things during our short lives here on earth—God and family. We need to let everything else fall where it may. God is being left out, and as parents, we will be held accountable for our children. Proverbs 22:6 (KJV) says, "Train up a child in the way he or she should go: and when they are old, they will not depart from it."

As far back as I can remember I used to sit in the swing on the front porch with my black nanny (Ms. Connie Randolph). While waiting for the horn to sound for the change of shifts at the mill, Connie and I would play a game to see who would spot my dad first as he was walking across the parking lot to the house. I didn't realize it then, but Dad must have had a hot job in the mill because he would be soaking wet from sweat when he got home. (That same horn used at the mill is now on display in front of the Clinton Museum on North Broad Street in Clinton, South Carolina.) I could easily watch for him because we lived so close to the mill that I could throw a baseball and hit it.

Ms. Connie would attend to my brother and me while my mom slept and my dad worked. Mom slept during the day because she worked the graveyard shift. Several years passed before I understood that my mom worked the third shift—at night—and not in a graveyard. Ms. Connie would cook and clean, and she was always in the kitchen canning food. You just don't hear about young girls canning stuff nowadays. To them, I think, canning now means quitting a job.

I understand Ms. Connie didn't charge much, because she would take home half of what she cooked and canned. When Ms. Connie died in 1960, I didn't understand why we were the only white family at her wake. It just didn't seem right. I didn't know there were problems between races. I learned later on in life about the race issue the hard way. We loved Ms. Connie as one of our family members. She cried when we cried. She cried when our parents spanked us. She really took care of us, as if we were her own. The color of skin didn't matter. It was the amount of love you had in your heart. Galatians 3:28 (KJV) states, "There is neither Jew nor Greek, there is neither bond nor free, there is neither male nor female: for ye are all one in Christ Jesus."

I don't think Ms. Connie was paid much cash, because I can remember seeing a pay stub from one of my parent's checks for about forty-five dollars. It was from the Clinton Cotton Mill, dated 1959. I guess that's why Dad had a second job at night during the week working at Yarborough's Filling Station on West Main Street in Clinton. He worked at Yarborough's at night when it wasn't dirt track racing season. I think the forty-five dollars was a full week's salary for an employee at the mill back then. I can also remember that our house payment was twenty-two dollars a month. That was a huge payment back in those days.

I can remember not having much and not asking for anything. I guess I learned a dollar's value at an early age. My brother and I didn't have a lot in those days, but we had the things we needed. Every year, we would make our annual trip to Laurens, South Carolina to Rosenblum's department store to get those awful brown brogans and two pairs of stiff dungarees to wear. The very first thing we did with those stiff-butted dungarees was to put them in the ringer washer on the back porch. We had to kick it to get it started and keep it running. For those who had one or watched the movie about Loretta Lynn's life entitled *Coal Miner's Daughter,* you'll know what I'm talking about. In the movie, she was playing music while washing clothes on the front porch; she had to kick the machine to keep it running. After a few hundred washings, those stiff dungarees would finally limber up. I can recall someone walking down a street and hearing those new dungarees make that sanding sound as their legs rubbed back and forth. I hated those dungarees and brogan shoes we got each year.

After a while, we finally we got our first pair of all-star tennis shoes. Man, were we so proud of those shoes! I think my first pair cost $3.95 plus tax. You cannot even purchase a pair of shoe strings today for $3.95. The rule was brogans for winter and all- stars for summer unless we went barefooted, which was the thing to do during the summertime. We now joke to others about how poor we were when Dad went to the filling station to get an old tire for us for Christmas. We would roll that old tire up and down the sidewalk every day. We wore it out in a year's time. You won't believe this. The very the next year, Dad had that tire recapped for us!

On our birthdays, our parents would give us a picture of a birthday cake torn from a magazine. Because we couldn't afford a cake, they would set the picture on fire, and we would blow out the picture and make a wish. We couldn't afford cheese for the rat traps, so we would place a picture of a piece of cheese from a sales paper on the trap for the rat. The next morning, there would be a picture of a dead rat beside the trap.

One Christmas, we couldn't afford lights and ornaments for the Christmas tree, so I improvised. Mom was taking several medications that came in different-sized bottles. I collected those empty bottles, painted them different colors, and hung them on the tree as ornaments. For paint, I used old finger nail polish and model car paint purchased at Rose's Five and Dime store. For garland, I linked together old beer and soda tops to form a long strand. Before the newfangled soda tops, they could be linked together to form a chain. I strung the chain around the Christmas tree. The painted medicine bottles and soda-top chain served their purposes. I thought it was pretty ingenious for a kid my age. The Christmas tree really did not look all that bad.

Photo by R.W. Page

CHAPTER 2

Early School Days

My first taste of public school was at M. S. Bailey Elementary. The mill company and the Baileys had donated the school, like most things in Clinton. It was located on Elizabeth Street in Clinton, South Carolina. If my memory serves me correctly, the school was about two miles from my house. Two miles doesn't sound like a lot, but to walk it every day in the cold and rain seemed like it took forever—especially in the first grade. Sometimes, I would take a shortcut between the old Cavalier ballpark and the Clinton cemetery. A narrow path between the fences separated the two. I would stop and read headstones on the way home from school. One stands out in my mind; it went something like this:

Remember, friends, as you pass by.
As you are now,
So once was I.
As I am now,
Soon you shall be.
Get right with Jesus and follow me!

That particular inscription was scary to a small boy walking beside a cemetery. It has been stamped in my mind for nearly sixty years. I now understand it more with each passing year. I would also try to determine who had been buried the longest at the graveyard.

The first grade was really the first time I saw my wife-to-be. It happened one afternoon as I was walking home from school. I passed by her house on Bailey Street as she was standing at her backyard fence. She was holding on to the fence with both hands, and she had on a diaper. As I was walking by, her diaper slid down below her navel, and it was at that moment I fell in love with her.

You don't see many kids walking to school, because now it looks like there is a yellow school bus stopping at every corner. I have ridden around the mill village several times of late, and I haven't seen any children walking to or from school. Again, perhaps it's because of the times we live in today.

Life at Bailey school wasn't all that great. I fought with a guy named David every day before, after, and during school. We fought so often that the principal, Mr. Horace Smith, appointed me to be one of the school patrolmen. Student patrolmen watched out for small kids, fights, and other potential problems. Actually, the patrolmen were tattletales, if you want to know the truth. During recess, I would take my patrol belt off and stick it in my pocket. Then David and I would resume our fight.

A few months ago, David and I ran into each another for the first time in over forty years. We started talking, and we spoke of those times at Bailey school. We laugh now about how silly it all was. He is living for the Lord, and I told him I was too. I wished him and his family well, as he did me and mine. When talking to folks you haven't seen in a long time, you find out that almost everyone has problems. I learned that it wasn't just me.

CHAPTER 3

Grammar School and Changes

Jimmy was one friend I had in grammar school. He and I were appointed the official popcorn poppers for the school. The teachers would let us out of class early so that we could start the popcorn popping. Man, I can still smell the popcorn aroma filling the halls of that small school.

At lunch recess, kids could come to what was called the *canteen* to purchase a bag of popcorn for five cents. That's where I got my first taste of entrepreneurship. Walking home with Jimmy after school, it didn't seem right that Jimmy had a pocketful of shiny nickels, and all I had was a pocketful of burnt popcorn seeds. Now, what's wrong with that picture? Jimmy still tells me every time he sees me that he is the only friend I have. But this old boy had a few more friends who became important later on in life.

Having to repeat the third grade was a really devastating experience. It hurt to see my friends move on ahead of me. Of course, I caught back up with some of them over the years, or they waited on me. I think that's where my problems with schools actually began. The third grade teacher held me back because I had a sixty-eight average in arithmetic. Nowadays, sixty is passing!

I can recall another story about a guy who went by the name of Joe. Joe acted as if he weren't all there from time to time, but he was smarter than most gave him credit for being. During a history class, I can remember (as if it happened yesterday) that the teacher called on Joe to answer the question, "Who took Bull Run?" That topic had been the homework assignment the night before. Joe wouldn't answer the question. I don't know if he hadn't done his homework or simply wouldn't answer. The teacher sent Joe to the principal's office for being disobedient. Mr. Smith, the principal, told Joe that he would have to bring one of his parents back to school with him the next morning, or he would be expelled.

The next day, Joe brought his dad with him to school. Joe's dad was furious because he was missing work. The principal explained to Joe's dad what had taken place in the classroom. He explained that Joe would not give the teacher an answer or even attempt to answer the question when called upon. Joe's dad asked Mr. Smith what the question was. Mr. Smith replied, "Who took Bull Run?"

Joe's dad looked at Joe and asked, "Joe, who took Bull Run?" Joe just stood there and didn't say a word. I could tell Joe's dad was really getting upset at Joe. Joe's dad said, "Joe, if you know who took Bull Run, tell them so they can get it back and I can go to work."

I watched the mill village change a lot over the years. I watched as the mill company expand the size of the cotton mill twice. I watched them make a parking lot out of our football field. I often wondered if things were moving too fast then and if the cotton mill should have stayed with what it originally had. I watched as the mill company actually moved several houses across the street from us, made a new street behind us, and named it Milling Street. I was amazed as they moved over twenty houses and watched those big houses being lifted up off their foundations

11

for relocation. I watched two-story houses off Sloan Street being moved to what is now called Elizabeth Street.

When the cotton mill was running at night, it was a sound that you listened for to fall asleep—a kind of humming that just put you to sleep. I miss that sound. When the mill stopped at midnight on Saturdays, man, it was hard to fall asleep! I didn't get a good night's sleep again until midnight on Sunday when the mill started back up. I wonder now if that's why it's hard for me to sleep at night. I had listened to the roaring and humming of that old cotton mill for eighteen years of my life. Nope, it just couldn't be that.

I had a lot of fun living in the mill village, but I also witnessed many tragedies that impacted my life. While the mill authorities were moving a house, I watched one man lose his life. The man reached up and grabbed an electrical wire stuck on top of a house as the house was moving under the wire. The man screamed to the top of his lungs and appeared to be on fire. Then his body went limp. What I saw that day would be hard for any child to deal with. No one knew I was having a problem with what I saw, but I had nightmares about it afterward.

Another tragedy occurred while I was watching for dad to come home from work. A car ran over a small child. My dad saw it happen, scooped the child up in his arms, and took him to the local hospital—the Blalock Clinic, I think it was. The child died, and it had a dramatic effect on all of us who witnessed it. My brother and I saw another child die who'd been hit by a car that ran a stop sign. That was the beginning of many life lessons I would experience and deal with alone. So while I was still in grammar school, I had already had three traumatic experiences that would haunt me for years to come.

CHAPTER 4

My Dad

Little did I know I would have such a short time with my hero, Dad. Dad wasn't a highly-educated man. He only had an eighth-grade education, but he was what I call a *do-ologist*. It seemed that Dad could do just about anything. I remember when he remodeled the kitchen one summer. I don't know if I was helping him or just getting in his way. Either way, it didn't seem to bother him. Without a miter box or many tools to use, he took his pocketknife and carved out all the miter joints. (A miter box is a tool used to saw angles on molding to join them together at a forty-five-degree angle.) His pocketknife was his miter box. My son now owns that knife.

I remember Dad fixing a knob that broke off the stove. We couldn't afford to buy a knob, so my dad carved one out of wood. He was also a "shade tree" mechanic. I've seen him start cars that most folks had given up on. I learned a lot from his *do-ology*.

He was always ready to help folks, especially the elderly and children. Dad would ride around the mill village and check on some of the older folks. One couple that comes to mind was James and Clara Crain. We all called them Uncle James and Aunt Clara. I really don't think we were actually related to them. Well, it didn't matter. I admired him for taking the time to check on the older people. I guess he bestowed that willingness on my brother and me, as we have done some of the same things with the elderly. My brother, Rick, still takes the time to look in on the older folks as his own health allows.

I can remember Dad always had old cars in the backyard; he worked on them and traded them for other things. One trade he made was for a couple of motorcycles. They didn't hang around the house long; he traded them for a couple of small Renault cars. I think Mom persuaded Dad to trade them in a nice sort of way. I don't remember how or what was said, because the persuading was so loud at times. The Renaults were similar in size to the 1969 Volkswagen. My brother and I learned to drive those cars while we were still in grammar school. To us, they were the most entertaining things in the world. We drove many miles around and around the coal shed in the backyard.

A coal shed? What? I know some of you will not recall what that is. For years, the mill houses did not have gas or oil for a heat source. Some folks had to heat with small fireplaces and burn coal for warmth in the winter. Each house in the village had a small wooden shed in the backyard in which to store coal. Thus, it was called a *coal shed*. We carried a lot of coal for heat back then, having to go out when it was freezing to fetch a bucketful of coal. Since my brother was the eldest, he can remember this better than I can. I do recall some mill folks saying they paid ten dollars a ton for coal.

Dad also made a trade for a pony. We really shouldn't have had this pony at the house, but I guess they didn't have the rules back then that they have now. That pony would break a chain just about every day while we were in school. Sometimes, we all would have to chase the pony around the mill village for hours until we caught it. I saw my dad get mad at that pony once, and he grabbed it around the neck. He actually flipped the pony on its back. Man, I thought that pony was dead! I only saw my dad get upset twice, and that was one of the times. We finally sold the pony and stuck with the Renaults for a couple of years.

We spent every Saturday night at the dirt track races when Dad drove dirt track cars for Mr. George Price. After work during racing season, Dad would walk across the backyard to Mr. Price's house on Milling Street to work on the racecar. As kids, we would tag along and get in the way. Driving a racecar was Dad's hobby for about eight years.

On the weekends, Dad would round us all up to pitch horseshoes. All the neighbors would gather in our backyard for horseshoe tournaments. That was the big thing to do back then. I bet we moved the horseshoe stobs at least ten times because of the holes they made over time. Dad didn't mind, because we all had so much fun.

The second time I saw my dad upset was the time when Mom called the mill around eleven-thirty at night to say she wouldn't be in to work on the third shift. It was snowing outside to beat the band (meaning, it was really coming down). That started it! The telephone rang, and Mom answered it. It was the third shift boss spinner. He told Mom that she lived within a few hundred feet from her work. (We actually lived even closer than that to the mill property.) She tried to explain to him that my dad had told her she wasn't going to work, because the weather was too bad. She interrupted the call by hanging up on him. About an hour had passed, and there was a knock at the front door around twelve-thirty in the morning. It was Mom's boss. He had made his way to the house to escort Mom to work. Dad went to the door and asked, "Didn't she tell you on the phone that she wasn't coming in?"

The boss began to explain something, but Dad slammed the front door in his face. About thirty seconds later, we all heard a loud scream and then a moaning sound coming from outside.

15

Dad opened the door, and the boss had fallen down the steps and broken his arm. Dad told him, "That's why she isn't coming to work!" He just shut the door and left him where he lay.

Dad was a firm disciplinary type. If he said no or stop, we honored his commands. It was always best for the backside to do so. If we didn't, we would get an old-fashioned striping. (They would call that child abuse today). I think I had enough stripes sometimes to be a general in his army. Every morning, Dad would wake us by saying, "Okay, boys, off and on," meaning, off your backsides and on your feet. It didn't take too many times for us to learn he meant it at the first "off and on."

One morning, Dad got us up for school and told me to cut the grass when I got home from school before I went out to play, but I forgot. That night, Dad gave me another promotion in his army. I got some more stripes before I went to bed. At daylight the next morning, I was cutting the grass before I went to school. Believe you me, I never forgot not to do it again!

Dad wouldn't let me or my brother fist fight each other, as most siblings did. He would make us wear boxing gloves and duke it out. The same thing applied to all the kids in the neighborhood; there was no fist-to-fist fighting. If you were going to fight, you had to wear the gloves. Over the years, my brother and I got pretty quick with our hands.

As far back as six years old, I remember a frightening experience with my father. I still have problems with what I saw. Early one morning, I recall hearing a loud noise coming from my parents' room. I jumped out of bed to see what it was. As I ran into their bedroom, there lay my dad on the floor, shaking. Later that afternoon, my mom tried to explain that Dad had what they called epileptic seizures. I saw this happen to him several other times, and those images have stuck with me until this day. I have a lot of compassion for people who live with this problem. It's something a young child shouldn't have to see.

Life, as we knew it, would change quickly, turning my world upside down.

On September 17, 1968, my father passed away from what the doctor said was stomach cancer. He was only thirty-seven. When Dad got sick, he didn't want my brother and me to know how bad the illness was. Rick was older, and I think he knew more than I did. I can remember being sent to Boy Scout camp while he was sick. I think I was sent there just to get my mind off of my dad's condition. While at camp, I can remember Dad walking up the mountain after his operation to visit me on parents' day. That was just one month before he passed away.

After returning home from camp, Dad wasn't getting any better. I remember seeing him fall to the floor coming out of the bathroom. I could tell Dad was really weak and sick. Little did I know that morning, when the ambulance came and took him away, he wouldn't return home alive.

At some point during Dad's sickness, he spent a few days at Bailey Hospital in Clinton, South Carolina before he was transferred to Self Memorial Hospital in Greenwood, South Carolina. The doctors didn't order the transfer, because Mom did that on her own. Mom could tell that Dad wasn't getting any better at the Clinton facility. Dad didn't go by ambulance; Mom took him by car. During the transfer to Greenwood, Mom pulled over to the side of the road because Dad began hemorrhaging. A highway patrolman happened to come by, and he saw what was taking place. He then gave Mom a police escort to the emergency room at the hospital. Lights and sirens were blaring as my dad was clinging to life.

About three o'clock in the morning on September 17, 1968, the telephone rang. It was the preacher from Friendship Baptist Church on highway 308 in Clinton. He had gotten a call from Mom to bring us to Greenwood Hospital. He instructed my brother and me to be ready because he was on the way to pick us up. He was taking us to see Dad because Dad was asking for us. We later found out that the doctors weren't going to let us see him, because they said we were too young. Mom raised the roof until the hospital finally allowed us in to see Dad. It was his final wish—to see his boys.

We went in to see Dad and spoke with him before he passed away later that morning. For some reason, my brother and I knew—when the telephone rang the morning of September the seventeenth—that it was going to be the last day we would see Dad alive. I had a sickening feeling in the pit of my stomach that morning. And it would not be the last time I experienced that feeling.

Dad had a perfect ten-year attendance record when he worked at the mill. When the mill company heard of Dad's death, I was told they stopped operations in the department he had worked in for about two minutes in his memory. That was awesome to hear! Over the years of talking to different people who knew my dad, I never heard a negative thing about him. I know he wasn't perfect, but to me he was perfect for the thirteen years I knew him. I know for a fact he loved his two sons.

Dad had left the mill at one point and had gone to work for a new company in Clinton called the Torrington Bearings Company. It is my personal belief that my dad's death was caused by inhaling some degreasing fumes from the job he was on at that company. Prior to my dad's death, Mom was laid off from work at the local E.L. Mansure plant. We believe to this day that it was because the company didn't want to pay for Dad's health and life insurance policies. I believe that because after Mom was let go, E.L. Mansure's business began a downward trend and finally went out of business.

Going to the kitchen and not having anything in the refrigerator or in the cabinets was a bad feeling for a boy who had just lost his dad. Just after his passing, I can remember a man from Dad's work, Mr. Ellis Huffsteadler, bringing us several bags of groceries. They called it a "pounding" back in those days. A pounding was when people would bring some cans of food and place them in a bag or box for coworkers who had been sick or had experienced a death in the family. I don't think people help each other out like that now. To me, that really is so sad.

With big business and corporations today, you are just a number to them. I experienced some of that in my own job. The tradition of family dedication to a company and the companies dedicated to the families is a thing of the past. It's my belief that big business should get back to Christ. To survive the stress of imports and the loss of jobs, we all need Christ back in the center of our lives and our work.

After Dad died, I had several offers to go make some after-school money. Mr. Robert Satterfield of Robert's Drive-in offered me a job. Mr. Frank Whiteford also extended me an offer of work. The offer I chose was to work at the Clinton Drug Store for Mr. Red Pinson. At fifty cents an hour, I was making big money. Well, at least it beat the morning paper route my brother and I had. Getting up at three o'clock every morning before school to deliver those awful papers was for the birds. It didn't matter if it was raining, snowing, or whatever. We had to deliver those newspapers. Just being late any morning would cause folks to complain. Folks in the mill village wanted their papers!

Red's was a local burger joint in the mill village just a block from my house. It offered short-order sandwiches such as hot dogs, hamburgers, and French fries. Some people would come in and place their orders, while others would call in their orders for takeout. We had one call-in order for twelve hot dogs to be wrapped in aluminum foil. When the person came in to pick up the order, Mr. Pinson asked, "Why the aluminum foil?"

The lady explained to us that her brother had enjoyed eating Red's hot dogs for the first twenty years of his life. He had moved away and was living in Dallas, Texas. The lady explained to us that she was leaving to visit her brother in Texas, and he wanted her to bring him some Red's hot dogs. I guess you can say that was the longest take out order we ever had at Red's. She returned weeks later to the store and said the people on the airplane wanted to know what that delicious smell was. She said the entire plane smelled of Red's hot dogs.

Mr. Pinson took me under his wing as an employee at the age of thirteen and let me work after school and weekends to earn money. I learned a lot about the public when I worked for him. You cannot satisfy everyone, no matter how hard you try. It's just impossible to do.

Red had a son who came in and pestered us all the time. He would get in the way when we were busy and laugh about it. When Red wasn't at the store, Red's son and I fought all the time. An older man Mac—also worked for Red. Mac always instigated the altercations between Red's son and me. On one Saturday afternoon, Red's son and I got into a fight outside the store. As we were fighting, I got the best of him. Red pulled up while I was sitting on top of his son, casually drinking an orange crush soda. I thought when Red got out of his car that my career as a burger flipper would be over, but it wasn't.

Mac was an ornery old man from time to time. (Well, most of the time.) Just a few years before my employment, while my dad was still alive, I must have upset Mac for some reason. He grabbed me by my throat and choked me. I went home crying and told my dad about it. After I went to work for Red, he used to tell me the story of the "choke hold." He said he saw my dad coming, and when he entered the store he could see fire in my dad's eyes. Red said he shouted out, "Jim, please don't kill him!" (Meaning, don't kill Mac.) After Dad got through with Mac in the back room that day, I never had another minute's trouble from Mac. But at that time, I did not know what had taken place.

During my first Christmas week at Red's, I worked over seventy hours. While I was working, I noticed all my friends were out playing with their new Christmas toys and presents. At that time in my life, it didn't seem to bother me, or I didn't think it did. I would go to school at eight o'clock in the morning, get out of school at three o'clock in the afternoon, and then go to work at Red's until about ten o'clock in the evening. Then I would go home to wait until it was time to get Mom up around eleven o'clock so that she could get ready for her job on the third shift. I would take her a cup of coffee and make sure she was wide-awake. Then I would take my bath and go to bed. The cycle would begin all over again the next day. I was given a lot of responsibility at the tender age of thirteen.

CHAPTER 5

My Brother's Motorcycle Wreck

While working at Red's, my brother, Rick, was involved in a motorcycle accident on March 23, 1969; he was hospitalized for several months. This accident occurred six months after my dad passed away. I had to quit school to help out at home and help care for him. Since my mom needed to be closer to the hospital, which was about thirty miles away, she decided to move us to Greenwood, South Carolina.

After a few months, Rick was released from the hospital, and we moved back home to Clinton. He was in a body cast from his chest down to his ankles for about a year. I can recall something that is funny now, but it wasn't back then. My brother was having some severe stomach pain, and I called the doctor. When the doctor arrived a short while later, he diagnosed Rick as being constipated. I never let on to the doctor that I didn't know what constipated was. The doctor gave me some medicine to give to my brother and left. I was to give Rick a suppository before he went to sleep. They were greasy, pointed little things, to say the least. It took several tries to get him to swallow those suppositories. They would melt before he got them down. I called the doctor back and explained what was happening. The doctor shouted over the telephone, "Wrong place, son, wrong place!"

I am here to tell you that I waited on Mom to administer the next dose. A lot of stress was put on all of us during this time, but it seemed we were coping the best way we knew how. As a young man of thirteen, I had already experienced enough stress to last a lifetime, but it wasn't over.

CHAPTER 6

Middle School, All Boys

As my brother got back on his feet after his terrible accident, we both got back into school. It was during the time local schools were being integrated. That first year, the school administration decided to put the girls in one school and the boys in another. At that point, the race problems began. As one of the biggest guys around, it seemed I was provoked into some kind of altercation every day. I had several altercations, but one was with a guy who went by the name Bug. He and I fought so fiercely that we both had to be helped to the principal's office. And it wasn't over!

After helping out a friend, Darrel Ward, who was being attacked because he was wearing a pair of designer jeans his mom had bought him, I was jumped by at least twelve guys, and chaos broke out. Police, South Carolina Law Enforcement Department, and school officials were all around the school the next morning. Several of the guys who jumped me were expelled, some were sent home for a few days, and others just didn't show back up at all. This wasn't what I went back to school to learn.

At my dad's bedside before his passing, he told my brother and me that there were two things he wanted us to do. One was to have patience in all that we did; the other was to finish school.

That was a motivator for me. I was making good grades and just wanted to get out of school. As for having patience, I am still working on it.

I crossed paths just a few years ago with the retired principal of Bell Street Middle School. He took me to his side and said that he had something to tell me. He said, "Ron, we used you to get things done at Bell Street Middle School that we couldn't do ourselves as teachers and administrators." Now, how sad is that? That was an eye-opener, if there is such a thing.

Later, I got a call from Washington DC from one of the guys with whom I had fought at Bell Street Middle School. He called me to apologize for causing all the altercations. He said because he was now a minister, he needed to get the past off his chest. He told me that he could not carry on with his work for the Lord unless he called me and apologized. He actually called me during his church service. All was forgiven, and we wished each other well. He was the second one to do this in the past couple of years.

A friend I worked with at Red's left and got a job at the local mill store. I applied also. I could tell that Mr. Reeder, the store manager, knew I wasn't yet fifteen, but he hired me anyway. I worked off and on for the Clinton mill store throughout my school years. I enjoyed my work there and learned to do a lot of things. I met many people and helped some folks when I could. I worked with Wayne and Claudette Power. They had two daughters, Kim and April. They were like family to me in the beginning. Later on, they would become my in-laws. The mill store was my comfort place.

I had several jobs during my career at the Clinton mill store such as bagger, delivery person, meat cutter, stocker, salesperson, and filling station attendant. During my time there, I earned money to buy my own clothes, shoes, and whatever else I needed. I guess, in a sense, I knew I was helping out at home in some way. I was told that when hard times hit the workers at the mill, the mill would pay employees with loonies. A loony had a value on it, and it could be traded at the mill store for needed items.

I may get in trouble for this one, but here goes anyway. There was an elderly lady named Ms. "V" who came into the store every Saturday afternoon just before closing. She would always call me "Wrestler." Ms. "V" said I looked like Ollie or Arn Anderson—a famous wrestling tag team back in those days. She had a son at home who was paralyzed from the waist down. She attended to her son twenty-four hours a day, seven days a week and had been doing so for nearly twenty years. She would always want twenty-five cents' worth of hamburger meat. Since it was almost closing time and we didn't keep the hamburger meat over the weekend, I usually wrapped up about three pounds for her and put a price of twenty-five cents on it.

Do you reckon I will get in trouble for that? If so, I have already asked the Lord to forgive me, and he is the only one who counts. I would tell her that when she was ready to check out with her groceries to let me know, and I would drive her home. She was about eighty years young, and she walked back and forth to the store. I heard she lived to be 104 years old. I miss Ms. "V." I miss the mill store people.

CHAPTER 7

High School Days

During my junior year of high school, I went out for varsity football. This would be my first attempt at learning organized sports. It took a while for me to learn not to closeline (tackle) players around their necks, as we did in the days of back-alley football. At least that is what my position coach, Jerry Lewis, taught me. In organized football, there are certain ways to block and tackle a player.

In a game between the Clinton Red Devils and the York Green Dragons, we were behind fourteen to zero at halftime. Our team manager, Mr. Sonny "Sweet Thang" Patterson, brought in some cold sodas for everyone during the break. The coach stopped him, grabbed a soda, and slammed it on a stool next to him. The coach then asked, "If anyone thinks he deserves one of these drinks, come up and get it!"

Looking around the room, I made my way to the front and took one. As I opened the soda, I said, "Coach, it's not my fault; I have not played a down of football!"

I had hoped the coach hadn't heard my remarks. The team went on to win that game by a score of 20 to 14. Boy, did I ever pay for that comment! After that year, I decided to go to work for my head coach, W. Keith Richardson. Together, we did different jobs around all the schools in the district. That may have been a mistake, looking back on it now. B.F. Shaw, a local pipe company from Laurens, South Carolina, donated a brand-new set of goal posts to the high school, but we had to have them installed. The local electrical company came out and drilled a hole as big around as a telephone pole and about six feet deep. As I was standing there watching the truck pull away after drilling the holes, I saw the coach out of the corner of my eye. He was wearing a smirk, which indicated he was up to something. (Some old footballers who played for Coach Richardson will know what I'm talking about with regard to that little grin of his.)

I noticed he was approaching the hole where I was standing. Derrick Wessinger was at the other hole. In the coach's hand, he had one of those green fold-up army shovels. You know—the kind of shovel that army soldiers use to dig foxholes. He grinned at me and asked, "Do you remember those remarks you made at halftime about the soda?"

He did remember! He was referring to the cold sodas when we were behind fourteen to zero at halftime during the York ballgame of 1973. I said, "Yes, sir."

He tossed the shovel over to me and said, "I want that hole six feet deep and six feet in diameter."

I am here to tell you that I dug that hole for days, using nothing but that little green army shovel. That was the payback I got for the soda comment. Coach Richardson has told me over the years that he and his family still laugh about the infamous hole-digging episode. He said it was a funny sight to see nothing but dirt flying up out of that hole.

I believe the hole I dug was off center by a couple of inches. So it might have been my fault that we missed a field goal that could have won the state championship title during my senior year of football. I couldn't put the blame on the kicker for missing the field goal by an inch or so. I learned more than just sports those two years I played.

I became very close to coach. I had no one who made me go to school. I just remembered what my dad had said about finishing school.

During my senior year, I decided that if I were going to put myself through practice again, I was going to be a starter for the Red Devils. All during that pre-season, hard work paid off. I became a starter until halftime of the first game of the season. Then I quit because of a decision my position coach made. He replaced me with another player. The head coach called me at home because I hadn't shown up at school the following Monday morning. I explained to him what had happened and the change that was made during the game; he told me to be in his office after school.

During the meeting with my position coach and head coach, the position coach said that he just wanted to give my replacement some experience. The head coach talked me into returning to the team. He said that if I came back, I would practice with the ends. I chose to return and practiced with the head coach the rest of my football career.

My football career ended on the last game of the regular season because of a head injury. I was so looking forward to the playoffs that year. I wanted to play against my old offensive line coach who had left to become the head coach in York, South Carolina. But it just wasn't meant to be.

I spent several days in the local hospital because of the head injury. The only good thing that came out of my hospital stay was meeting my wife-to-be for the second time. (Remember, the first time I met her, she was in diapers.) She was the prettiest candy striper that I had ever seen. We didn't start dating until two years after this encounter.

The year before my football career ended, I had a car wreck on my way home from school when the steering broke on my 1964 Chevy. I had centered the car into a telephone pole and spent several days in the hospital for that too. My head seemed to be the focal point for injuries early in my life.

During my senior year, I went on to play track, as I had the two previous years. I wanted to letter in track, especially as a senior. After a track meet, the managers would load the equipment onto the bus, and we would get on and head back home. During a meet in Woodruff, South Carolina, the manager loaded a twelve-pound shot put on the luggage rack inside the bus and did not secure it. As we approached the highway going down the hill from the school, the shot put rolled off the rack and hit me on top of the head. It knocked me out cold for a few seconds. The legendary local high school coach, Willie Varner, saw the bus suddenly stop, and he rushed over to see what was wrong. He realized that I was knocked out and began to shake my head back and forth, asking me if I was alright. I told him that I would be if he didn't break my neck by continuing to shake it.

I was really mad, not because of the shot put or the coach, but because of what the doctors had said about my football injury. They explained to me that if I received another blow to my head, it might kill me. I just don't think anyone in a football suit would have hit me as hard as that shot put did, and I survived that. Looking back, maybe I could have finished my football career after all. I guess that is why some of the guys called me "Shot Put Page."

When I was a senior in high school, I got the manager's job at the Quick Way convenience store in Joanna, South Carolina. I was told by the district supervisor that I was the youngest manager employed by the company. After graduation, I spent most of my time at Quick Way getting the store up to the company's standards. After spending June through mid-August 1975 there,

I made a decision that working all those hours wasn't my cup of tea. I quit my job at Quick Way, but left it in the best shape it had been in for quite some time. I made another career change.

I went to work for the Kaywood Company, which manufactured wooden house shutters in Joanna, South Carolina. My job there was to pull orders in the shipping department for customers such as Sears, J.C. Penny, and other large retail stores. My career ended with Kaywood after only two weeks, due to the car accident I was involved in on August 31, 1975.

CHAPTER 8

The Wreck behind Presbyterian College in Clinton, South Carolina

Photo by Rick Page

Late at night on Sunday, August 31, 1975, I was involved in an automobile accident. A regular group of us was hanging out at Rocky's Texaco that night as we did every Sunday. Mike Johnson had just gotten a brand-new 1975 Rally Camaro. He had stopped by several times to show it to me and wanted to take me for a cruise before he went home. Mike Johnson, Joe Cothren, Mitchell Scott, and Randy Humphries had been riding around all day. They had returned to Rocky's that night to take me for a spin in Mike's car around ten thirty. When the guys arrived back at Rocky's, Mitchell got out, and I got in on the passenger's side. Mike was driving, Joe was sitting behind him, and Randy was behind me. We left Rocky's and never returned.

We headed south toward the C-mart, made the circle through the parking lot, and headed back toward Presbyterian College on South Broad Street. At the red light at South Broad Street and East Maple, we made a right turn. There were no streetlights along the roadside of East Maple and large hedges lined its banks. Those banks and hedges caused blind spots as we approached the first curve in the road. The roads were covered with loose stone and tar.

We approached the new library on the Presbyterian College campus and rounded the curve. It looked as if a car had stopped in the middle of the road; its headlights were on high beam. As Mike attempted to brake, his car skidded sideways, and the other car hit us on the driver's side door. Mike and Joe died at the scene, I later found out. Seven people were involved in the wreck—the four of us in Mike's car and three college students in the other car. I had in my mind the idea of jumping out the passenger's side window just before we collided. After the crash, I was hanging halfway out the window. Some guys from the college ran and lifted me out of the car and placed me on the road just behind the wrecked car I'd been in.

Photo by Rick Page

There was a lot of confusion at the scene. I kept telling them to take me home because I thought I was okay. I smelled a heavy odor of gasoline coming from the car, began to panic, and couldn't breathe. I was lying directly behind the car, which was too close to the gasoline coming from the ruptured gas tank. I was screaming for them to move me from the behind the car. I looked up and saw one guy I recognized. His name was Claude; I had gone to high school with him. Claude was attending Presbyterian College. He later told me he had been at the new library studying and had heard the crash. Claude and others ran toward us to see if they could help out. I remember reaching in my pocket for my money. I had just gotten paid on Friday and had not spent much. I recall telling Claude to give the money to my mom. At that point, I didn't know how much I had. But somehow months later, I told my mom the exact amount.

It was chaotic at the crash scene as people began to gather. There were only two ambulances in the county of Laurens at the time. Shelton's Ambulance Service was the only company serving the county. The police and the highway patrol, once on the scene, called for Child's Funeral Home and Gray's Funeral Parlor to send out hearses to help. Years later, one of the ambulance attendants told me that the ambulance service and one of the funeral home companies were arguing over who was going to transfer whom and for how much. This took place while the injured needed urgent attention.

Officer Lieutenant Wright Simpson lived on South Broad Street, approximately 600 yards from where the accident happened. He said that he heard the cars hit while he was getting ready to go to work on the third shift. He walked to the crash site on foot. I was informed that while the people were discussing costs at the wreck scene, Lieutenant Simpson jumped into an ambulance and drove me to Bailey Hospital.

At the hospital, it was chaotic also. People were gathering as the news of the accident was spreading around the small town of Clinton. People, friends, and family members were asking questions but getting no answers. Nothing from inside was being broadcast to the outsiders, mainly because the families of the injured and deceased hadn't been contacted. Cars were parked in the way of emergency vehicles. People were gathered in the driveways. As family members arrived, they couldn't get by the cars and the crowds. Some of the local police officers had to do crowd control and remove some of the cars.

I never lost consciousness during the time I spent at Clinton Hospital. It seemed as if I had been lying on the gurney for hours, but it had only been a few minutes. I looked up as they brought someone in covered up on a stretcher. Coach Bill Rhodes and Coach Keith Richardson had arrived about that time. I asked Coach Rhodes who was covered up, but he wouldn't tell me. He tried to say it was no one I knew. I told him I would get up and look for myself it he didn't tell me. He saw I was becoming worse by trying to get up. He finally leaned down and told me Mike didn't make it, and I went to pieces.

They took me into x-ray, and I was cursing and telling them to transfer me to Greenwood Hospital. While I was in x-ray, my mom showed up. Mom saw Mike and thought it was me. Mike and I both had beards and dark hair. Mom became so upset that she had to be sedated. The doctors and nurses calmed my mom, told her I was still alive and holding my own, and that I was currently in the x-ray room. I was rolled out into a hallway outside the x-ray room for a short time. I have no idea why. I think it was because I did not have the external injuries that others had. So the doctors and nurses thought I wasn't hurt as badly. After the doctors read the x-rays, they stepped it up a bit.

Standing there was another person I knew, but at the time I just didn't remember who it was. I found out later it was Tim Entrekin. He told me I was cursing everyone out and wanted to go to Greenwood Hospital. He knew all of us, but he was already at the hospital because someone in his family was having a baby. Years later, Tim and I talked about that night, and he explained to me how bad it really was at the hospital. He said I had no visible injuries, so at first they were in no hurry to treat me. Once they returned from the x-ray room, they moved a bit quicker. The x-ray had confirmed that all my injuries were internal. I can remember signing my own permission papers to be transferred to Self Memorial Hospital in Greenwood, South Carolina.

As I was reloaded into the ambulance to be transferred to Greenwood, I turned and looked out of one window and saw nothing but cars and flashing red lights. As I looked out the other window, I saw a friend standing there with tears coming from his eyes. It was Jack Herman Veal, Jr. Jack and I were good friends during our school days.

Clinging on to life and seeing Jack, I had a flashback of when he and I played as football teammates against Hanna High School. Hanna was a class 4A school, and Clinton was a class 3A. We went to Hanna High School in Anderson, South Carolina to play its team and beat Hanna 2 to 0. After the game, the Hanna players and fans were so mad they wanted to fight. Jack and I were the two biggest players on our team; we both weighed over 250 pounds. As we took up positions to defend ourselves, Jack's mom—Ms. Pearl—came rushing onto the field and stood in front of both us. She weighed a solid ninety pounds but shouted out, "Don't you hurt my babies!" As the ambulance began to pull off from Bailey Hospital, Jack's eyes made contact with mine. I tried to give him thumbs up. I miss old Jack.

No one knew if I would survive. My folks and friends were told that it didn't look good for me. During my ride to the Greenwood Hospital (located some thirty miles away), the roads were being resurfaced, which didn't help. Dr. Walker and the emergency attendant, John O'Neal, rode in the back of the ambulance with me because my injuries were worse than originally thought.

On arriving at Self Memorial Hospital in Greenwood, the doctors began to cut me, while I was still on the gurney, in order to shove a chest tube into my side. This happened even before I entered the hospital. People said the folks on the third floor heard me scream out in pain. The doctors later told my mom that my pain index had already peaked. I was rushed into surgery, and they were cutting and prepping me at the same time. They were running out of time, as one doctor later put it.

Because I had multiple internal injuries, the operation lasted over twelve hours. I had a ruptured spleen, which had to be removed. My left lung had collapsed. My stomach had burst. My diaphragm was split in half. Some of my intestines were damaged and had drawn up into my diaphragm. Almost everything internally was drawn up into my chest area. A trauma team of five doctors worked with me. I was revived twice on the operating table. After the surgery, I was placed in the critical care unit to be monitored around the clock.

As I was lying in the critical care unit, I overheard the doctor tell my mother to get my family together. Yes, I really heard the conversation as it took place. He told her that it looked very grim and that I would most likely not make it through the first twenty-four hours. Because my mom was so upset, the doctor put her in a room next to me.

My brother, Rick, was stationed at a naval base in Meridian, Mississippi at the time. Since it was a holiday weekend and he was in service, they had to get in touch with him through the Red Cross. He was at a friend's house, where they were having a Labor Day weekend get-together. He said that his friends pitched in, brought him some coffee, and got him ready to make the trip to Greenwood, South Carolina. He told me that he never drove under 100 miles per hour during the trip back to South Carolina. I remember him looking at me once as I was going in and out of consciousness.

Because my condition remained critical, the nurses began packing me in ice as my fever rose to 105.2 degrees. I was also on life support machines, but I still heard people around me talking. A lot of visitors came into the room. I was seeing folks and relatives I hadn't seen in years. It seemed as if I were lying in a coffin as they passed by me. I tried to talk to them and tell them I would be okay, but I couldn't utter a word. As I lay there, again I overheard the doctors tell my mom to call the family back in.

At that point, my room filled with such brightness, and standing at the foot of my bed was my great-great grandmother. She had passed away when I was about ten years old. She said, "Come with me, son. You are going to be alright."

I don't know if I dreamed that or not, but it seemed vivid and real to me. I remember my great-great grandmother wearing her hair in a bun, as most Blackfoot Indian women did in her day. That night, her hair was long and flowing. Was my great-great grandmother my guardian angel? Was she God-sent? Was it just a dream? Was it the medication I was on? I haven't the answers, but I knew when she left my room that I wasn't going to die.

Rick stayed with me at night during the critical time after my surgery. He would go home, take a bath, and return to be with me. On his way back to the hospital, he would go by Red's in the mill village to buy a couple of hot dogs for himself and his wife. They would take the hot dogs to the back of the room and eat them. By going to the back of the room, they thought it would not bother or disturb me. They were eating the hot dogs right over the air conditioner vents. He said that the air conditioner blew the smell of the hot dogs over to me. Rick said I suddenly sat straight up in bed, turned my head back and forth, and sniffed the air. Rick told me that Red's hot dogs saved my life. I talked with the ambulance attendant, John O'Neal, years after the wreck occurred. We both worked at the Torrington Company in Clinton, South Carolina. Some fifteen years after the event, John asked me if I had been one of the guys involved in the accident behind Presbyterian College in Clinton. I told him yes. He then said he needed to get something off his chest. He told me that he had been the attendant who rode in the back of the ambulance with the doctor and me. He went on to tell me that the doctor said to tell the ambulance driver to slow down. The doctor told John there was no need to be in a hurry because I wasn't going to make it to Greenwood alive. But God had other plans for me.

CHAPTER 9

Recovery Time

During my stay in the critical care unit, several preachers visited me. Before they left, they would pray for me. They would be thanked and would go on their various ways. There was one preacher who came into my room and started preaching. He told me that I was going to die and go to hell. He laid out his Bible and began shouting. My brother was staying with me, and he just turned away. I got so upset at the preacher that machines started ringing, alarms started going off, and lights began flashing on the machines I was hooked up to. It wasn't long before all the nurses on my floor came running into my room. My brother explained to the nurses what had just taken place with the preacher. Needless to say, the doctors banned the preacher from my room.

Family members said that I was asking for a certain girl by name as I came in and out of consciousness. When I got to the point where I could talk and see, I noticed that someone had contacted the wrong person! No need at this point to name any names. It would just upset some folks, and that is not my intention in telling my story.

At this point, I would again like to thank my doctors, Dr. Stewart, Dr. Stephens, and Dr. Holloway of the Greenwood surgical team, for putting me back together. I would also like to express my thanks to my family, the nurses, and most of all, my Lord and Savior Jesus Christ.

If you are a young adult, I hope you can realize that what happened to us that night could happen to any one of you at any given time. I am so blessed that my God spared me and gave me a second chance. So, young people, keep your eyes on the cross. Please understand that if you just go for a ride with friends, it could be your last ride. Don't let the hearse be the only ride that takes you to church. Moms and dads, it is your responsibility to take your children to church until the age of accountability. Yes, you will be held accountable for your children when the Day of Judgment comes.

While I was recovering, I did a lot of reflecting. We all have plenty of reasons to praise God. In Psalms, David gives believers a list of things for which to praise God: his forgiveness, healing, redemption, lovingkindness, tender mercies, providence, righteousness, justice, grace, and patience.

We receive all these gifts from God without deserving them. No matter how difficult life's journey is, you can always count your blessings—past, present, and future. When you feel you have nothing to praise God for, read David's list in the book of Psalms. Psalm 103:4 (KJV) states, "Who redeemeth thy life from destruction; who crowneth thee with lovingkindness and tender mercies."

At that point in my life, I was seeing and remembering things I hadn't thought about in several years. All the medical doctors had given up on me. Yet I am here today telling my story. It is by the grace of God. There is no doubt in my mind that the Lord touched me that night. (This was not to be the last time God touched my life. God would lay his hands on me two more times! I will speak of those events later.) There was a purpose bestowed upon my life.

It wasn't long after my great-great grandmother appeared before me that I was asking to go home. A few weeks passed, and all the doctors agreed I would do much better at home. One doctor stated that it was a divine healing. One doctor said he wouldn't have given two cents for my life, and he performed the surgery! He may have been the physician, but he wasn't the *Great Physician*. Amen!

The rumors were really flying around town. No, we were not drinking; no, we were not drag racing on East Maple Street. As for the stories of us using drugs and weed, no, we were not doing that either. Those who knew me knew how I felt about drugs. Rumors were being spread that I had died. People were calling the hospital continuously. Mr. Gray, the funeral parlor director, said he got so many calls about me that he called the hospital to check on me. After finding out I was still holding my own, he took his telephone off the hook. I don't know if having a funeral parlor director call and check on you is a good thing or not!

It must have been very difficult during the first weeks and months of the new school year. Mike Johnson and Joe Cochran, the two students who died in the wreck, had played football at Clinton High School. The players dedicated the season to their memories. That year, 1975, Clinton won another state championship.

During practices, the late Mr. Louie Webb told me that Coach Richardson wanted a regular update on my condition. Mr. Webb passed away in the summer of 2013. I miss him greatly. Over the years, I enjoyed talking with him at the football games and at church. Rest in peace, my friend.

Even though I had already graduated, the coaches were still concerned about me. That goes to show how being a teammate follows you the rest of your life. You learn more than just the game of football. You learn a lot about the game of life.

The night of the accident, someone stole my car and my eight-track tape player. They did this while all of the turmoil of the accident was taking place. What makes it so bad is that I know who that person is. I have talked to him many times over the years and wondered how he can face me. Instead of me being my old self and taking matters into my own hands, I am letting the guilt eat away at him, my "friend." I have forgiven him because if I hadn't, God would not have forgiven me.

The guy who was supposedly hurt the worst in the other car called me the day I got home from the hospital. He wanted us to meet and talk about what happened the night of the accident. I told him that I knew what had happened and that he should never set foot in front of me!

I think about Joe and Mike a lot. I never will get over their untimely deaths. I can still hear them now shouting out in the halls of Clinton High School, "Daddy Ron!" Randy Humphries, the other surviving person in the car, had several broken bones including a fractured jaw; he remained at Clinton's Bailey Hospital the night of the car accident. He did check out on his own to go to the funerals of Mike and Joe.

As the years passed and our bodies began to heal, our paths crossed around 1990 when I started attending Davidson Baptist Church in Clinton, South Carolina. Randy and I had never talked after the night of the wreck fifteen years earlier. He had been attending Davison Street Baptist Church for some time and was studying to be a minister. I told him how proud I was that he had been called to become a minister. But I could tell something just wasn't right between us. After several encounters feeling the way I did, I had a chance to sit and talk with Randy. He began to explain to me what people were saying about me. He was told that I had sued Mike's family because of the wreck. I assured him that never happened. He said he had bad feelings toward me from listening to people, and he was avoiding me. As we talked and I explained what really took place, he apologized and began to tear up. I told him he knew better than to listen to rumors; when there is a conflict like this, he should always go to the source.

Both Randy and I became deacons at Davidson Baptist Church. We had many talks over those years and we became close once again. The best part is that we became brothers in Christ. He and I keep in touch as much as time allows us. (We ask that you continue to pray for us and the families involved because we are still dealing with this tragic event every day of our lives.)

This part of this story about the accident is dedicated to the memory of Mike Johnson and Joe Cothran, with special thanks to Rev. Randy Humphries, Claude Crocker Jr, Officer Wright Simpson, Jack Herman Veal, Linda Darby, W. Keith Richardson, and Bill "Old Man" Rhodes. I would also like to recognize my other friends who stole my car and tape player! I would like to thank Ms. Linda Darby, one of my teachers who visited me at home. These visits really meant a lot to me during my recovery.

As I began to get my strength back, I asked my team of doctors if I could drive my automobile. I really began to get cabin fever. I was told I could drive short distances around town. On my first day driving, I went to town just to look around and view the scenes that I hadn't seen since the accident happened. While driving back toward my house, I was driving down South Broad Street, passing by Presbyterian College. In front of me was a white-paneled van from the Southern Bell Telephone Company. As we approached the stop light at South Broad and Maple, the light changed to red. The van stopped, and I stopped directly behind the van. The van had on the right-hand turn signal to turn onto West Maple. As the light changed to green, the van proceeded to make the right-hand turn. As I approached the stoplight, the van suddenly made a quick left turn right into the side of my car. I panicked! This was the same road I had the accident on just a few months before. Flashbacks overtook me at that point, and I just became helpless. Someone had called my house for help. To this day, I cannot recall who came and took me home. I didn't have any injuries, thank God, but I did have some bad flashbacks. Several weeks passed before I could drive again. I just could not fathom being in another wreck so soon on the same road. It's been forty years, and I have not been down East Maple Street since that second accident occurred.

CHAPTER 10

Back to Work

The time came when I felt better and just had to get out of the house. The walls were closing in on me. Soap operas were beginning to engulf me. The doctors permitted me to go to work part time, as long as I didn't overdo it. There could be no heavy lifting, and I needed to be able to take a break when I became tired.

I returned to the Clinton mill store as a salesperson in the dry goods department. The Clinton mill store appeared to be the crutch in my life. This was the second time the store had been good to me by giving me a job. I already knew the job and people, and I really felt at home there. Times were changing for the store; more people had started going to the new strip malls to shop. During this time, the mill folks started learning how not to depend on the Clinton mill store for their needs.

The Clinton mill store is where I began to see my wife-to-be, Kim. She had developed into a beautiful girl. She had a smile that would illuminate any room. As a senior in high school, I used to regularly sit on the radiator in the hallways and watch her as she passed by. I would flirt with her a little as she approached me. Since she knew I would be at that particular place, I often wonder if she just happened to walk that way by chance. With me would be two friends, Johnny Thomas and the late David "Myrtle" Campbell. As Kim was coming down the hall one day, I said, "Here comes my future wife."

She had a boyfriend at the time, and I remember telling him that I was going to take his woman. Later, I was told he got mad, hit the wall, and broke his hand. Kim was not the tomboyish type she had been several years earlier. I really started to notice her. I already knew her from being around her folks at the store and visiting them at their home from time to time. Her father, Wayne, was the store's assistant manager, and her mom, Claudette, worked in the same department where I worked.

After school each day, Kim would come by the store; she said she wanted to visit her parents. Yeah, right! I would always make sure I was at the store that time of day. I would be putting bikes and such together near the back of the department where I worked. Kim would always get change from one of her parents to purchase a drink. As she walked toward the drink machines, we made eye contact and smiled at each other.

During the Christmas season of that year, Kim got a job at the store wrapping Christmas gifts. (Little did I know that we would be married in a couple of years, and she would become one of *my* greatest gifts.) During a break from wrapping gifts, Kim made her way over to the spot where I was working. We began to talk, and she asked me why I hadn't been around her house lately. I don't remember my reply, but I showed up the next weekend. (I later found out that she had broken up with her boyfriend.)

A few weeks before, I had helped her father enclose the carport for a game room. I hadn't been back since finishing the job. For some reason, Kim wouldn't come out to see me on my first couple of visits. Around the fourth visit, she began to come outside by the pool where we all had gathered. I got up the nerve to ask her if she wanted to go riding in my car for a little while.

She said yes. We went riding several times after that and began to see each other on a regular basis.

After she graduated high school, she began to attend Presbyterian College, and I went to work at the Torrington Company in January 1977. We got married in January 1978. That was one of the highlights of my life.

During my time at the Torrington Company, I worked for a guy named Joe Parks. I met him while playing football for the Clinton Red Devils. Joe was the public address announcer for the Red Devil's home games. I was hired to run a lathe—a metal turning machine. Since I seemed to have a talent for working on the various machines in the department, during my breaks I would train myself to set up the machines and became skilled at doing so.

The time I spent training myself paid off. A machine set-up job opened up on the second shift, so I applied for the position and got it. It paid a little more than what I had been making. The increase in pay was welcomed because Kim and I needed more money. There was always too much month at the end of the money! As with most newlyweds, we needed all I could earn. I was the only one working, and she was going to Presbyterian College full-time. It seemed we lived off of Kraft macaroni and cheese dinners for years. (You know the ones I'm talking about—five boxes for a dollar.) We had those dinners any way Kim could fix them: with the cheese, without the cheese, or with meat, when we could afford it. They are now and always will be banned from my house.

I was on the first shift before long, and that helped us out. While I was at work, Kim was at school. I helped around the house in the evenings while she did her homework. I would get up for work many mornings, and Kim would still be up studying from the previous night. I didn't have much to offer my new bride, but we were happy. After thirty-seven years of marriage, I tell folks that we are still on our honeymoon.

I had a single-wide mobile home on my old home place there in the mill village a year or so before we got married. It was okay for a starter home. As our family began to grow, we looked for another place. While Kim was still in college, God blessed us with a wonderful daughter we named Michelle Dawn Page. For the first seven years of her life, Michelle was the only grandchild on both sides of the family. She was spoiled rotten to the core! She got things from grandparents, great-grandparents, aunts, and uncles. Michelle was (and still is) daddy's little girl—no matter how old she is or how upset she gets with me.

Kim and I found a house we could afford at 516 North Broad Street in Clinton, South Carolina. Man, we loved that house! It was built well by Mr. Collie Anderson for one of his daughters in the 1950s.

Kim finished college early (as she had high school), and she began her teaching career at Bell Street Middle School in Clinton at the age of twenty. People always teased me that she almost became my teacher because I had turned twenty just after graduation from high school. I didn't think it was as funny as they thought it was.

For some reason, I thought it was once again time for a career change. The decision turned out to be a big mistake. I was making decent money on the first shift at Torrington, and Kim was working as a teacher at Bell Street Middle School. But after four years, I left my job at Torrington for one at the Michelin Tire Company in Spartanburg, South Carolina on April 25, 1980. They offered me more money to start. I learned a valuable lesson: money isn't everything when it comes to your job. You need to be happy at what you are doing.

The job I was hired to do at Michelin got mixed up. The man who hired me went on a leave of absence. When I reported to work, the personnel department had assigned me to another guy.

49

The departments went by letters such as OPK, OPL, OPT, and so forth, not names. I was assigned to a machine operator's job instead of a machine mechanic's job—the one for which I'd been previously tested and hired. One measly letter screwed me up!

I spoke with the personnel department, and they acknowledged that a mistake had been made. The personnel department said it was company policy to stay on the job for six months before transferring. Even the guy who hired me apologized to me when he returned to work. He said that he could do nothing until after the six-month period. I realized driving thirty-five miles one way and working swing shifts just wasn't cutting it for me. Since my employer would not do anything about the mix-up, I would.

A new company was coming to Clinton, just six miles from our house. It was called the Mueller Company, and it manufactured large water and gas valves. I made more money at Michelin, but I wasn't happy. I knew Michelin wasn't going to transfer me off the machine operator's job, because my group was setting all kinds of production records. I applied for a job at the Mueller Company and was hired. I left Michelin on August 22, 1980 after only four long, hard months there. I learned a lot but hated the job.

Before I left Michelin, I had an exit interview with the personnel department. They asked me if I knew any guys who wanted a job and worked as hard as I did. I presented them with five names, and they hired all of them. I believe four of them are still working there. The Mueller Company hired me on September 23, 1980 at just fifty-one cents an hour less than I was making at Michelin, and I didn't have to drive an extra sixty miles a day. It was a wise move for me.

While at the Mueller Company, I learned how to run computer-controlled machines and really enjoyed the work. Most places call them CNC machines, meaning, computer numerically controlled. I was being trained by the Japanese technicians and was also learning about the machining centers and about Japan's culture. Things were looking better for me at the Mueller Company. I had learned how to operate computer-assisted lathes and large machining centers. I received several promotions in a short period of time, but then Torrington came calling.

I had heard that Torrington was having trouble training guys on how to set up the machines and keep them running—the ones I'd had four years'experience setting up. At a local sports event, Mr. Russ Emerson, the plant manager, asked me if I would be interested in coming back to work at Torrington. It didn't take long before he and I reached an agreement to return.

When I told my supervisor at the Mueller Company that I would be working a two weeks' notice, I also agreed to help train someone on the machine that I was running. I felt obligated because the Japanese technicians had already returned to Japan. I told my supervisor I would help out and not leave him stranded. The supervisor said that would be okay. I called Torrington and explained what had taken place. They told me to come to work the next day.

After six months with the Mueller Company, I returned to the Torrington Company in April 1981. *This was the beginning of something good,* I thought. But was I ever wrong!

I returned to the position at Torrington that I had left a few months earlier. From the onset, I knew that my job was going to be shipped to another plant in a year's time. It wasn't that I was better than anyone else on the setter's job, but it was the fact that I kept good notes on the machine settings. I still had my notes on the machines when I returned. The company had workers hand-drilling holes in parts that automatic machines were designed to drill, but the machines wouldn't run the parts. It was costing the company big money to hand-drill the parts, and only about 200 could be drilled by hand per hour. The machines were designed to run about 2,000 parts per hour.

It took me a couple of days before I had everything up and running. The plant manager and department managers were happy to see all the machines running parts again.

The agreement was that after my job was transferred out, I would go to the machine shop, which had a machine just like the one I was trained on at the Mueller Company. It was my understanding that the computer lathe (called a J&L lathe) wasn't producing parts as well as it should. The shop was the start of many uphill battles for me; they lasted more than fifteen years, until I transferred out.

CHAPTER 11

Work Battles

The Torrington Company went on short time when the economy took a turn for the worse. The production part of the plant began a four-day work week. It didn't take long before the four-day work week hit the support departments such as the machine shop. Being the lowest in seniority in the machine shop, I was preparing myself for a layoff. I began looking for another job. I was already working a security job part-time to make up for the one day of work I had lost. The foreman later told me that I would be okay because I was one of two employees who had knowledge of and experience with the machine, and production had increased over 300 percent on the lathe.

The foreman also let me know that the plant had too much training invested in me and the new machine to lay me off. Well, the guys in the shop didn't like it a bit. Some of them had over twenty years of service in the shop, and they were being laid off. It sowed discord among the shop associates. I could tell it really upset them because I was getting the cold shoulder from a lot of the guys. The plant management later realized it had made a big mistake because it took a lot of time and money to train machine shop personnel.

The plant manager said that if another plant-wide layoff took place, the machine shop associates would be the last to go. After a while, the plant brought back several of the guys, but others had moved on to other jobs. Some had bitter tastes in their mouths because of the way they'd been treated, and they wouldn't come back. Until the day I transferred out of the machine shop, some of the guys still held a grudge against me for what had happened.

After a couple of months, I requested a transfer to the third shift so that I could attend Piedmont Technical College to further my education. The department superintendent approved my request. My going on the third shift didn't sit well with some of the guys either.

I started Piedmont Technical College while working the third shift. I made note cards to study by and taped them to my machine. I traveled back and forth with Gene Pinson. He and his dad were still running Red's, the local burger joint in the mill village. I would pay for the gas, and Gene would drive so that I could sleep going to and from school. My wife said a couple of times that I almost drowned myself falling asleep while in the bathtub. From time to time, she would hear me gurgle as I fell asleep sliding down in the tub.

Gene's dad, Red Pinson, became sick and passed away during our last year at Tech. I asked Gene what he was going to do. He'd already closed the store and had gone to work at the local Radio Shack in Clinton, South Carolina. During our ride home one night, I asked Gene if he wanted to reopen Red's. He said he didn't have the funds. I told him I didn't either, but we could raise the necessary capital to do it. I explained that if he would put up $200.00, I would also, and we could raise the rest of the money. He said that I was crazy, but he was game.

Gene and I finished Tech with business degrees in 1985, started a small flea market business, and worked every weekend for a year. We would get to the flea market at four o'clock in the morning just to get a spot on the inside of the market. We also worked at the fair one week to raise funds. Friends would pass us by and laugh and call us *carneys*.

Gene and I took the money we made and started remodeling his dad's old store. We had made a deal to purchase the property from Gene's mother. I was working full-time at Torrington and had been promoted to the first shift, and Gene was working at Radio Shack. We would get off work, go down to the building, and work until midnight. Some nights, we would work past midnight. We would get up for work the next morning and do it all over again.

On November 13, 1985, God blessed my wife and me with a son. Kim had her hands full working five days week as a teacher and taking care of a newborn and a seven-year-old at home. My wife hung tough while supporting me in my endeavors. Both of us were hoping it would pay off for our family in the long run. Gene and his wife, Ann, were also hoping that this was a good move for both families to reopen Red's.

I felt really bad about spending so much time away from my family. But I wanted them to have more than what I could give them on a salary from Torrington. The day finally arrived for us to open the doors of the newly-remodeled Red's Burger Masters. We kept the name of Red's and added Burger Masters to it. Red's Burger Masters was born on April 14, 1986.

We didn't do any advertising, because we wanted to start off slowly. Man, were we not prepared for what happened when the health inspector gave us the thumbs up to open! Kim was off from school, and Ann took a day off from her job. Gene had quit Radio Shack to stock the new store and get things ready. I took a day's vacation, and we had hired a couple of young boys to help out.

When we turned the open sign on, folks were lined up for three city blocks. We ran out of food three times. We had so many meal orders that we had to take the telephone off the hook. Kim ran the cash register while we all cooked and made up the orders. We didn't stop until eleven o'clock that night. We just couldn't believe what had happened. I told Gene it was a good thing we hadn't advertised! After checking the sales that night after we closed, we had only a ten-dollar mistake. Business was so good that day that we had to have a police escort to the bank's night deposit box.

Gene and I really loved dirt track racing, so we used the business to help sponsor two local race cars. Ronnie Brookshire owned one of the race cars, and J.D. Oakley owned the other. Both cars looked great with Red's Burger Masters' label down their sides. We put as much money in each car as we could afford from the profits of Red's Burger Masters. Gene and I felt this was a good way to advertise the business. It paid off because we gained many customers from the Laurens area.

We both also loved the Clinton Red Devils and cooked for the whole team several times a year. We would close the store on Friday nights around seven o'clock or seven-thirty to go to see the Clinton Red Devils play. The news of our closing the store got out somehow to Charlotte, North Carolina. *The Charlotte Observer* newspaper couldn't believe that two businessmen would close a restaurant just to go to a high school football game. They sent a reporter down to the store to write a story about us. We made the front page of their sports section.

I was really enjoying my job, even though there still were some guys who had hard feelings about me being in the shop. I can remember when a major part broke on one of the big presses in a department that stamped out production. The inoperable press was costing an estimated $1,500 an hour. Torrington had contacted the manufacturer of the press, and they said that it would be months before they could get the necessary part and service the press.

After talking to my machine programmer and the supervisor, we decided that we would attempt to make the part. It was a large part, about three feet long and about ten inches in diameter. It was threaded on one end and had a large round ball on the other. Since the company didn't have the material in-house to make it, Torrington flew its own plane to Alabama to get it. Meanwhile, the programmer and I were readying the machine to make the part. We worked a solid eighteen hours straight after receiving the necessary material. The part worked, and the plant manager was very excited about what we had accomplished. He said that I would always have job security with the Torrington Company.

After the success of making the part, the foreman and I talked about my becoming the programmer of the machine I was running. He told me that my job classification would go up and would mean earning more money. Little did I know that he had already cleared it through personnel for me to jump ahead of the guy who had more seniority on the machine. I refused to take the job under those conditions. That decision didn't sit well with management. I told them that I had enough problems with people in the shop, and I didn't need any more. They offered the guy with seniority the chance to be the programmer. He said that he would like a chance to learn it. After several weeks went by, the guy said he didn't want the job and that he wanted off the machine altogether. He was reassigned to the manual engine lathe in the machine shop.

I began to learn how to program the computer-assisted machine and went to class to learn the ins and outs of programming. After about a year, I finally felt comfortable with the programming job. The engineer who had had the job was assigned to a new job, and I began to program and run the machine. I was also training a new operator on the machine. After the new operator became knowledgeable, I asked for the classification pay change because the shop foremen had said that I would get a pay raise. Time and again, I asked; he kept telling me that personnel would not okay the promotion. I asked him, "Why would I want to take on more responsibility for the same money?"

I explained that I would rather just operate the machine or, in other words, go back to the way it was. He said that programming was now a part of my job description. I appealed several times to the superintendent and personnel but got nowhere. I made the decision to do the bare minimum. Right or wrong, that's what I did, and I will stick to my opinion.

At that time, the plant was introducing the total quality management concept of team work. Every time they needed someone on a team or someone to go to a meeting, I volunteered. I lost interest in programming and running the machine. I felt that management had dealt me a bad hand in the machine shop, and I had a bitter taste in my mouth.

I remember an older guy called me over to his job and said, "I know they (management) have done you wrong big time. It's just like city hall. You cannot win or beat them at their games."

That gentleman gave me good advice, which I will take to my grave. He said to always operate under the systems already in place in a company or any organization such as Torrington. In other words, tell management what it wants to hear. If the company wants you on a team, join it. If the company wants you to take a trip, take it. If the company wants you to sit in a two-hour meeting and do nothing, then do it. That really wasn't the way I approached things. I always gave a 110 percent, but while I was still in the machine shop that was the protocol I worked under. At that point, I wanted out of the machine shop.

CHAPTER 12

The Selling of Red's Burger Masters

I was working at Red's (sometimes until midnight) and working full-time at Torrington; this schedule was really taking a toll on me. Gene could tell that it was playing havoc with my health and my personal life. My fuse was beginning to grow short. Gene also knew I had my plate full with several personal problems.

A gentlemen and his wife came by the restaurant one evening as I was working outside the store on some land we had acquired for extra parking space. I noticed them getting out of their car, but I kept on working. The woman went inside, and the man came over to where I was working. He asked me if Red's was for sale. I said jokingly, "Everything I have is for sale at the right price."

We talked for a while, and his wife came outside. I noticed she nodded her head at him. He asked me how much I would want for the restaurant. I asked, "Are you serious?"

He asked, "How much?"

Well, I knew what the business was doing, so I suggested a selling price to him—thinking he wouldn't buy it. The gentlemen reached into his pocket, shuffled out several large bills, and asked, "Will this hold it until we can get the papers signed?"

I said, "Hold on a minute. I have a partner inside with whom I need to discuss this."

We went inside, and I called Gene to the back of the restaurant. I asked him if he wanted to buy my part out. Gene told me that he didn't and asked me what was going on. I asked him if he wanted to sell the restaurant. Gene said that if I were selling, he would sell too. After telling him the offer amount, Gene said that we needed to sell. After four years of owning Red's Burger Masters, we sold. From time to time, Gene and I have spoken about having no regrets of selling the business. We were glad that Red's was continuing with its history.

Gene and Ann moved to Laurens, South Carolina with their new set of twins. We spoke to each other at least once a week by telephone, but times changed and we seemed to become too busy to stay in touch. Even emails became sporadic. Gene's two teenage sons really kept him busy.

I have never forgotten the good times we experienced while operating Red's Burger Masters. We hired one kid for part-time work. We both fired him about twenty times. All of the guys who worked there while they were in school have all become successful adults. I am very proud of each one of them. Thanks for the memories from Red's Burger Masters. I miss all of the customers and the talks we had over the years.

CHAPTER 13

Life after Red's Burger Master

After selling Red's Burger Masters, my wife and I started building our dream home. The house was completed, and we moved in during August 1990. At the same time, Kim became sick. I knew something was seriously wrong when she hadn't been Christmas shopping in the weeks preceding Christmas. Kim and I had just put all of our extra cash into the new house. She was beginning to miss many days from work because of her illness. Like most couples, we were a two-paycheck family.

Kim began to go to several doctors. None of them could pinpoint or diagnose her problem. She went to several specialists in Columbia, South Carolina, and they couldn't diagnose her problem either. She went to several more doctors in Spartanburg, South Carolina, with no luck there. I took her to specialists at Duke University in Durham, North Carolina, and they didn't help. Finally, we went to see Dr. Paul Cheney in Charlotte, North Carolina. He had become famous for diagnosing Legionnaires' disease at Lake Tahoe, California some years before.

He was expensive, but I was willing to spend whatever it took to have Kim well again. Doctor Cheney charged $3,000.00 a visit, and he did not accept insurance. Kim was diagnosed with what was known as chronic fatigue syndrome and fibromyalgia. The doctor explained to us that there were ten symptoms a person would have to have to be diagnosed with chronic fatigue syndrome. Dr. Cheney said most patients have no more than three of the ten symptoms, but Kim was found to have seven of the ten symptoms. Kim had to give up teaching, which devastated her. She also had to quit teaching at church. Dr. Cheney didn't think that she would get any better or any worse. He explained to us that, with the right kind of treatments, she could learn to live with the disease.

It would always upset Kim when folks would say, "I get tired also." It's not the same kind of tiredness that you and I would get from working. People with chronic fatigue syndrome may rest or sleep for days and still not be able to function well in their day to day activities. Kim had other health problems, but to look at her you would never know it. She always thought of others and never lost her smile.

I did not realize it, but the stress in me was building up. I began to find myself visiting the gravesites of Mike and Joe on a regular basis. These were the two guys who died in the car wreck I'd been involved in years earlier. Sometimes, I wouldn't even remember how I got to the graveyard or how long I stayed. Something was going on inside my head. I would go to work, come home, do the housework, and make sure the kids were fed and taken care of. I tried to take all the responsibility off Kim.

One particular afternoon, with all the stuff going on inside my head, I just started out the door. No one knew what was on my mind or what I was about to do. No one knew but the good Lord. As I was getting ready to leave, a car pulled into the driveway. A man got out; it was J.D. Shiflet, the pastor at Davidson Street Baptist Street in Clinton. Kim and the children had visited there several times; I had also visited a couple of times over the past two years. The preacher and I talked for a while, and he said that he didn't know why he stopped at that particular moment to visit. I told him that I knew why. The Lord had sent him my way! I confided in him what was on my mind.

Pastor Shiflet knew that I was upset and that I had a lot of stress. I wasn't dealing with the stress as I had been able to do over the years. I was thinking about my dad. I thought about my brother coming close to losing his life. The situation with my mom wasn't what it should have been. I felt that the car accident deaths of my friends, Mike and Joe, were my fault. My wife's health had begun to decline. My job was really bothering me. (Don't take this out of context. I wasn't blaming anyone for my problems, but my plate was too full!) Pastor Shiflet and I talked a little while longer, and that afternoon I surrendered my life to God. I felt a peace come over me that I hadn't felt in a very long time. Pastor Shiflet baptized me on May 16, 1993. The following verse demonstrates how I received this gift: "That if you shall confess with your mouth the Lord Jesus, and shall believe in your heart that God has raised him from the dead, you shall be saved" (Romans 10:9 KJV).

CHAPTER 14

Helping Others

I had been teaching myself auto-cad while I was still in the machine shop. Mainly, it was to keep my mind occupied and off all my personal problems. I would spend my breaks on the computer with the tutorial and learn as much as I could about computer drafting. I really enjoyed learning auto-cad. I did pretty well at it, if I say so myself.

I began to help Tim Entrekin draw up plans for a new church. The First Pentecostal Holiness Church had begun the process of relocating and building a new church. I spent many hours with Tim drawing the floor plans for the new church building. It wasn't long afterward that the drawings were ready and ground was broken.

After finishing the new church a few months later, the congregation held a day of dedication. I had asked Tim to let me know about the date because I wanted to be there. Little did I know that they were going to recognize me! I did not help them out to be recognized. I did it because I felt led by God. I could help save the church a lot of money and use my newly-acquired talent to do some work for the Lord. It was a new skill for me, and I wanted to share it. The congregation presented me with a certificate of appreciation on June 14, 1996.

About the same time, Pastor Tommy Padgett of Full Gospel Assembly, located behind the Lydia Mill community, had also started a new building plan. We spoke often at work and shared thoughts about our beliefs in the Lord. He knew that I was learning how to use the computer to draw building plans and asked me if I would help out. I told him that I would.

He and I started taking breaks together and laying out the floor plans for the new sanctuary. Each set of plans took almost three months to draw and get them to the point where the builders could use them. Pastor Padgett and his church members did most of the work on the inside. During the building stage, I would stop by from time to time and help out as much as possible. The folks at Full Gospel started calling me *deacon*. Although I was a member of Davidson Street Baptist Church, I would attend some services at Full Gospel Assembly and First Pentecostal. I enjoyed some of the ways that the Pentecostals worshipped the Lord. So I became a *Bapticostal*. I really don't believe in the different denominations. When I am asked what my affiliation is, I say Jesus Christ.

Pastor Padgett and his congregation also recognized me during their day of dedication on November 2, 1997. Again, that is not why I helped out and drew the church floor plans. I was just glad I could use my talents to save the church money. I attended Full Gospel Assembly several times, which is also a Pentecostal church, and really enjoyed its way of worshipping the Lord. I visited a Pentecostal camp meeting twice and enjoyed that. I don't care what affiliation you are. You just need to go and visit a Pentecostal camp meeting; I guarantee that you will be blessed!

God had touched me a second time with *his grace* on that day back in 1993. Pastor J.D. had been sent by God, and no one can make me believe otherwise. I later became baptized and joined the church. Times were good at church, and it really helped me out of a bad situation during a low time in my life. After a couple of years, I became a Sunday school teacher and was voted in as a deacon. Becoming a deacon was a proud moment in my life. We had eleven deacons at church during my time on the board. Another proud day was when the deacons honored me by voting me in as chairman. I think that was the first time I was selected or elected for anything in my life. Pastor J.D. asked me to give my testimony during a revival service at church. I tried to think of several ways or excuses to get out of it, but I couldn't refuse. Remembering how the Lord had touched me twice, I just couldn't let the Lord down.

Standing in front of a church body is a difficult thing to do. First of all, I didn't belong behind a sacred pulpit. In my book, a pulpit is holy ground. I don't like standing in front of crowds. After my testimony, Kim told me that she knew God had his hands on me because I spoke fluently and used correct English. I was asked several times to give my testimony at other churches. Young kids and adults came up to me and thanked me. They said that my testimony touched them in a special way. I explained that it was the Lord speaking through me and that he was the one who touched them. I could not do any of that on my own. That wouldn't be the last time God would bless my family and me.

As far back as I can remember, I thought a lot about the Lord and church. Growing up, we were sent to church on Sunday mornings, but we never attended together as a family. I loved to listen to gospel music. Even when I wasn't living for the Lord, I would listen to gospel music. It means more to me now that I've been saved. Sometimes at home, sitting beside the lake in my rocking chair, I listen to gospel music. My own health problems hinder me from attending church as regularly as I once did. I still listen to preaching and gospel music as often as I can. Man, I miss being at church. I miss the fellowship. I miss the people!

CHAPTER 15

More Drama

With all that was happening and had already happened on my job, I began to realize that my career with the Torrington Company needed a boost and a change. I had been checking on some colleges that offered night classes. While I was running my machine one day, Mark Entrekin walked up and began talking about going back to school. I said I was ready to do that too, and we started inquiring about several nearby colleges that offered evening classes. After several months, we discovered that Limestone College, located in Gaffney, South Carolina, offered classes and would even come to our job site. Mark and I, along with several others, enrolled in Limestone College under the new block program, meaning, we covered one subject—from the beginning to the end of the book— in six weeks. College was really demanding, but I was making great score

It was during this time that Brandon, my son, was playing little league baseball at the local YMCA. (Please don't get me started on the infamous "Y"!) I would attend as many games as I could to watch him play. We only had classes every other day, so that freed up some time for baseball watching.

The first year Brandon played, he made the all-star team as first baseman. As any parents would be, we were very proud of him. The rules stated that every all-star player must play at least one inning during a game. In the first game, everyone played but Brandon. I didn't get to watch the complete game that night, because I had an exam. My brother, Rick, was at the game watching what was taking place between Brandon and the coach.

As I was approaching the field, the game had just ended. I saw my brother walking with the coach toward the outfield. People were explaining to me what had just happened. I was told that Brandon did not get to play even one out of baseball—much less an inning—as the rules stated. I could tell that Rick was upset, and the coach was very upset and nervous. I can only imagine what Rick said to him.

After I got Brandon home, the telephone rang; it was Brandon's coach. He was actually crying on the phone. He said he was afraid that my brother was going to hurt him. He explained to me that he was going to start Brandon the next night. I told him not to do us any favors, because of what he had done to Brandon. I have always taught my kids that they are in competition with themselves and no one else. I taught them always to do their very best, and good things will happen.

I could tell the situation was really bothering Brandon. He'd earned the right to be on the all-star team, and he deserved to have playing time. I found out later that the other first base player was the coach's son. He already had one son on the team. That had never been alright with me. Just because the coach is a dad of one of the players shouldn't automatically entitle his son to be on the all-star team. I have seen it happen time and time again. Brandon kept his head up and got to play for a while during the games. As young as he was, he was a better person than I would have been. I couldn't have taken it as well as he did. It wouldn't be the last time I would see this young man's character in action.

The very next year, Brandon had a good baseball season. He played first base, pitched, and played catcher. There wasn't another player on his team who could play three positions. Brandon was the kind of player who did whatever it took for the team. Brandon was again playing for a coach who had two sons on the team. One son was a good athlete, and the other one wasn't as good.

It came time again to pick all-star players. The coaches and committee members were inside the YMCA choosing players before the last regular game of the season. I was outside watching the teams warm up. A friend of ours, who was an umpire at all the games and was on the selection committee, came up to me fuming. He explained to me that they did not pick Brandon for the all-star team. Our friend was really upset about their decision to pass over Brandon. He told me that Brandon had the highest on-base percentage, the most hits, the highest batting average, and played three positions. He told me that the coach's two sons made the all-stars. He explained that the coach could select two players from his team, and he picked his own two sons, which took up both slots. Brandon again was disappointed, but he kept his chin up. He said it was their loss, not his.

It's funny as I look back. All those coaches' kids from all those teams were on the local high school baseball team for two years. They had a record of something like three wins and forty-five losses. So much for the YMCA and its all-stars! I just don't like that organization. It's like any other business; it's all about the money and who you know. It appears to me that they have taken the Christian part out of the YMCA altogether.

The plant was implementing a new department and posted several new jobs on the plant-wide job posting board. As I wrote earlier, I wanted out of the machine shop. I became interested in one of the jobs, and I applied for it. I had to go through several interviews and write a paper on what I could contribute to the department. After three interviews, I was offered a job as an IPM Coordinator. IPM stood for integrated process management. In other words, we were going to use computers to keep up with the different variables of part manufacturing. Mostly, we were going to collect the statistics on a part and help to better manage the process.

This was an implementation team. It meant that once the job was over we would have the option to go back to our previous jobs. Knowing the company as I did then, I asked the personnel employee who interviewed me to put this information in writing. I was referring to the part about once the job was over we could return to our previous jobs. She hadn't been with Torrington long and said this was the first time anyone had asked her to put something in writing. I explained to her that Torrington had a history of promising and forgetting things. (Remember the job change classification that I didn't get?) I was reminding myself about the programmer's job in the machine shop when I was promised a raise and different classification, and they forgot about this promise.

The change felt good, and things started getting a bit better for me at the company. Several of us finished school and got our four-year degrees. I was especially proud of my degree and the 3.89 GPA I maintained. I graduated magna cum laude, but I really thanked the Lordy!

I was preparing myself for my new job change. A friend of the family came up to me while running my machine and training a new guy. He had worked for the company for years and had been a good friend of my dad. He had worked his way up to the front office by this time. He came over and said, "Ronny, I need to get something off my chest."

I asked, "What is bothering you?" I was not prepared for what I was about to hear. He and I discussed what may have contributed to dad's passing. After the discussion was over, I just broke down right then and there over that conversation. I was having feelings I hadn't had since my dad's passing. It didn't take long for the news of me being upset to hit the front office, and I was summoned there. I was seated in a vacant office with closed blinds. I was being questioned as to who said what and what was said. The effort of really trying to find out who told me about the chemicals failed. I wouldn't tell anyone. Others were sent to see if they could get me to talk. I told people they were wasting their time because I wasn't going to say who told me about my dad. I had made a promise. To this day, I have kept that promise.

I sent for and have received reports from the Department of Health (DHEC) that revealed there was evidence of the chemical trichloroethylene in the ground and in the ground water on that site. I am still having a hard time coping with this information. I also found out there are over 100 wells to monitor the ground water there.

It reminds me of the Erin Brockovich movie that aired on television a few years ago about the operations of a plant (PG&E) that caused cancer clusters. Julia Roberts played the attorney's assistant. I believe that if you worked at the Torrington Company, you should have a free screening of your health. I feel that I should do something, but what? A lot of people used the chemical at our plant to wash their hands and wash down their machines. It was called trichloroethylene[1] and it is very carcinogenic. I also used some of this solvent when I began working there. It was typically used to wash down machines and hand tools. Many of the people exposed to trichlororthylene have poor health. It makes me wonder if the chemical is the root cause of all the illness.

[1] Kleinfeld,M. and Tabershaw, I. R.:Trichloroethylene toxicity. Arch. Ind. Hyg. Occup.Med.,10:134,1954

CHAPTER 16

New Plant Manager

As the new plant manager came on board and started assessing all the service jobs, my job was about to change. After two years of integrated process management, the new manager wanted something different. I was on leave, having my gallbladder removed, when I found out that my job was changing. I had also completed a supervisor's course, which the plant had offered for new supervisors.

On my first day home from the hospital, my boss called and wanted to know if he could meet with me. I agreed to his request, even though I did not feel like it at the time. He and my new department manager came to my home and explained that we were doing away with integrated process management, and we were becoming product line diagnosticians. As a diagnostician, I would be in charge of problems within the process and scrap parts in my assigned departments. There were four of us, and the plant was divided into four product lines. While I was at home recuperating, the announcement of the diagnosticians went plant-wide.

On my first day back at work, my new superintendent called me into his office. He explained to me about my new job and went over my assignments. He said that my salary was being redlined. Redlined meant that I would not get any more salary raises. Being from the machine shop, I was the highest paid diagnostician in the department. My new superintendent's actions came across as being negative. I said that I would not accept the redlining of my new job and that I would go back to the machine shop. My previous superintendent was out on vacation, so I told my new superintendent that I would wait for his return. He told me that he was now my boss and what he said went. Well, that didn't sit well with me. I walked out and said I was still working for my old superintendent.

When my old superintendent came back to work, I explained to him what had taken place. He told me that it was not what was discussed before he left to go on vacation. He said that he would take care of it.

Personnel got involved. I heard the personnel manager page both superintendents, and about thirty minutes later, they paged me. A friend passed the personnel office and overheard my new boss say, "I hope this is not going to be an unruly meeting."

I thanked my friend for telling me this before I went into the office. As I was taking my seat, I looked at my new manager and the personnel manager and said, "This will not be an unruly meeting if I can help it."

I would have given anything to have had a picture of their faces when I said that. We began to discuss my situation, and they explained that I would be redlined. I told them that it was just like cutting my pay. In other words, they were going to let the other three guys' pay catch up with my salary, which was a pay cut for me. I just could not come to terms with that, so I said I would go back to the machine shop. My new boss said that was not an option. I smiled and pulled out the paper the woman from personnel had signed at my request two years earlier. Again, their chins hit the floor. They said they would get back to me, and I left.

On the following day, I was paged again to come to the personnel office to meet with my new boss and the personnel manager. They said that if I remained a diagnostician, my pay would go on as usual. This meant that if the plant workers got a raise, then I would also get one because I was already on top pay for my classification. They also told me if I stayed and accepted the diagnostician's job, the letter I had would become null and void.

I thought about it and accepted their terms. It was a good thing I had the letter! It pays to be prepared. The personnel woman later spoke with me and said she understood now what I was talking about when I had asked her to put my transfer in writing. Not long afterward, she was transferred to another plant. I always wondered if it was because of my letter.

I had just finished the supervisor's class at the plant and a couple of assignments that went along with the class. I filled in for a couple of foremen and supervisors while they were on vacation. I had an excellent rapport with one superintendent on my job assignment. I was also scheduled to take the Brown test. It was a psychological profile that was given to all supervisors and foremen before they were given a promotion. Robert L. Brown, PhD was the man who came up with the testing, which is known throughout the United States. Dr. Brown administered the test to me. It took two days and lasted about six hours each day. It was the usual type of testing with inkblots and putting square pegs into round holes.

After finishing the test, I had to sit down with Dr. Brown and go over my weak and strong points. The test identified what jobs suited an individual. He said that I did pretty well and was in a high percentage of people who make good leaders. The only negative thing he said was that it showed evidence of deep internal depression. He asked me if I drank a lot of sodas and tea. I told him that I did, and we let it go at that. I have always wondered if that was a sign of things to come in my life or if it had to do with my past. Maybe I should have followed up on that diagnosis then; maybe I wouldn't be in the shape I am in now.

After the battery of testing was over, I received several supervisory job offers. I felt that I could help the company out in this capacity. It wasn't the job title, as some may have thought, but it was the fact that I would be able to help people. I went through another round of interviews with the personnel department and was offered a supervisor's job on the third shift. I had to take a couple of days and talk this over with my wife. The third shift was a big change in our lives. After working the last twenty years on the first shift, this was a major decision we had to make together.

Another mistake in my life was in store for me. I had asked the foreman of the department about the workload and how supervision worked if weekend hours were scheduled. He said that I might only work one weekend out of the month. Kim and I weighed the pros and cons and decided to give it a go. Boy, did the foreman set me up!

I became the third shift supervisor of a department with sixty-five female and five male associates. I have never heard so many excuses to be off from work. I was the only supervisor on the third shift, but the other shifts had two each. My shift maintained the production levels, just as the first and second shifts did. I was proud and was making good progress with the associates. I had started weeding out the bad apples, and the others saw that I meant business. I wasn't going to put up with any nonsense, nor was I going to engage in favoritism. I explained early on that I wasn't in the department to babysit anyone. I said that I didn't care if they took extra break time, as long as the production numbers were where they needed to be.

I had a couple of people test me—just because I was new—but it didn't take long for them to get in line with my standards. One guy transferred out of the department because he didn't agree with the goals and directions I had set for the whole department.

After two weeks, he called me and asked if he could return to his old job. I told him if he could get the personnel department to okay it, I had no problem with his coming back. I knew personnel wouldn't let him come back. Even though I needed him and he was a good machine setter, he and I just didn't see eye to eye on things.

Working the third shift was a mistake for me. The foreman misspoke about working one weekend a month. We worked seven days a week from the time I took the job. I had gotten too old for the graveyard shift. I wasn't resting well and couldn't sleep in the daytime. I became hard to live with at home. The graveyard shift was making me grouchy, and I would get upset and fly off the handle over things that never used to bother me. It was having an effect on my kids. The third shift began to work on my health, and I knew that something had to be done.

I had already been working with the third shift superintendent on a plan to change the department, make it better for all associates, and increase production. We had far too many associates on each shift. With the right number of people, we had enough machines to make the production schedules. My third shift superintendent told me that he and I were getting flack; some felt that our plan was going nowhere and that we were wasting our time. During our breaks over a four-month period, we both worked on the plan and layout. We continued to hear rumors and negative comments about what we were trying to accomplish. No one had even seen the presentation and layout to comment on. I think it was just a lot of talk from the rumor mill.

To my surprise, the plant was adding a fourth shift to our department, and they needed a supervisor for it. The job was on Saturdays and Sundays from six o'clock in the morning until six o'clock in the evening. This would be better than the graveyard shift anytime. I applied and got the job as the fourth shift supervisor.

My knee and back had begun to bother me after a couple of months on the new shift. I visited a local orthopedist, and x-rays showed that I had a torn ligament in my right knee. The doctor said that I needed an operation, so I scheduled one. I hated to be out of work, but the knee was getting worse. I explained my situation to the manufacturing manager of the plant, and he agreed that I needed to go ahead and have my surgery. He said that my health came first. I was scheduled to be out of work for five weeks.

While I was on leave for the surgery, the third shift superintendent made our presentation about the recommended departmental changes to the plant manager, the assistant plant manager, the corporate vice president, and the district vice president of the company. Every one of those gentlemen approved what we had recommended. It was all implemented. Even though I was out on leave, I attended the presentation. The managers gave us nothing but praise for our hard work and were looking forward to the changes. However, I never got to see our plan in action.

While I was still recovering from knee surgery, my back began to give me problems. I'd had lower back pain over the years, but it was getting worse. I mentioned my back problems to my doctor during one of my visits. He said that while he had me out on medical leave, he needed to do an MRI. (An MRI is a type of scan of the spine and lower back. It is more precise than a regular x-ray.) As luck would have it, the MRI showed a compression fracture and spinal stenosis. My doctor said that my working days were over.

I guess it was alright for a grown man to cry because I broke down in his office. I just couldn't believe what I'd heard. I had worked since I was twelve years old, and sometimes I worked two jobs. I wanted my family to have the nice things: a good home and a better way of life than what I'd had. I was really depressed and went into seclusion. I would not answer the telephone, and I didn't want to talk with or see anyone.

CHAPTER 17

Supporting My Kids

While I was still out of work, I continued to try to support my children as they played sports. My son, Brandon, had just started junior high football when I began working the third shift. He was a good-sized player and really had a love for the game. Being on the third shift gave me enough time to sleep and to watch him play and practice.

Over the years, I went to just about every Clinton Red Devil's practice. Even when the Red Devils had a bad season, such as a two-win and a nine-loss season, I still went to the practices. Many times, I was the only person watching the Clinton Red Devils practice, as opposed to the years when they were winning. When the Clinton Red Devils were winning, there would be ten to twenty and sometimes as many as fifty spectators watching in attendance. I made it to every one of Brandon's middle school football practices. Even though I felt bad most of the time, I was determinedd to be there to support him. I knew how it felt not to have anyone from your family present to watch you play or even practice a sport. My father couldn't watch from the stands, because he had gone on to be with the Lord. My mom couldn't have cared less. My brother attended as often as possible when he was on leave from the military.

The one thing that hurt me the most as a player during my junior year was when the football team had parents' day. Parents' day was when the parents of the football players would sit on the sideline and be recognized during the halftime festivities. I remember as the team left the field during parents' night at halftime, I glanced over to where the parents were sitting on the sideline, and there were two empty chairs. The chairs had two tags on them marked *Page*. The feelings I had then just cut through my soul, as if a knife had pierced my heart. No young person should ever have to experience a moment like that. I made up my mind that night that if I had children, I would support and be there for them if they played any sport—even if I had to be carried to a game or a practice in the back of an ambulance.

I watched my daughter play volleyball and perform as a flag girl in the high school band. I even sat through a ten-hour band competition to watch the Devil Regiment Band perform. I also watched my daughter hit herself in the head with a flag. Ha!

Brandon became a pretty good player and was the starting center during his seventh, eighth, ninth, and tenth grade years. Brandon became what was called an eight-quarter player during his sophomore year. An eight-quarter player could play with the varsity team on Thursday nights and then again on Friday nights. Brandon even got the "Hustler" award his sophomore year at the local high school. It was an award given to a player for his ourstanding play as a team-player.

CHAPTER 18

Helping Out at High School

I had been in the press box for about fourteen years and decided, since my health was declining, to give it up. Making the climb up the steps to the press box was hard on me. Sometimes, it would take me twenty minutes to make it to the public address box. My job was to be the spotter. I would spot who made the tackle and relay it to the public address announcer who, at the start, was Joe Parks. Joe retired after doing the job for twenty-five years, and I got a friend of mine, Mark Entrekin, to take over from Joe. I knew that Mark had the gift of gab. After a couple of weeks, he would make a good public address announcer. Along with Mark and his brother, Tim, I took over the duties in the press box. We had some good years together. We enjoyed doing it for the kids and had fun among ourselves many nights. If one of us messed up in our duties, we would blame one of the others.

One of the most memorable nights occurred when we introduced the new Clinton Red Devil's mascot. The Booster Club had purchased a red devil suit, and it came with a large red devil head. The Booster Club also wanted to have smoke when the devil made his appearance during the game.

I decided to help out the first couple of times with the devil mascot's introduction. We got everything ready and started the smoke as the devil came out on top of a large platform where everyone could see him. I had on a wireless microphone so that I could communicate with him from the press box. As the mascot came out, I started the smoke machine. All of the smoke went inside the large devil head. I heard the guy in the suit start to cough, gag, and choke. I told the devil to make some noise! In a low voice, he began to growl like a tiger, thinking the fans could hear him. I told the devil that the people couldn't hear him. I began to laugh uncontrollably. Mark came on over the two-way radio and asked what the problem was. I said that I had a *sick* devil. I heard all of them in the press box begin to laugh. You could see the spectators turning and looking up at the press box at Mark and the others inside. Man, it was hilarious! It was hard for Mark to do the next several plays over the PA system. He laughed so hard that it took him a while to gain his composure. So much for the introduction!

Brandon had a close friend on the football team named Brian Sanders. Brian became like a brother to Brandon. They began to hang around with each other and encouraged each other on and off the playing field. Brian would come and spend the weekend with Brandon on Lake Greenwood and really enjoyed himself. I will yield here to my son's story and the article by Dave Pickren, "Profiles of Courage," dated February 10, 2004.

CHAPTER 19

Profiles of Courage: Clinton's Brandon Page

Dave Pickren

Every year, we watch as the top high school players in South Carolina sign their letters of intent for college. Every year, we hear a story about a young man signing scholarship papers and it makes us realize why high school football is such a great game. This year, we were introduced to Brandon Page from Clinton High School, who is headed to Presbyterian School.

September 10, 2002 is a day Brandon Page would like to forget. It is a day that the entire town of Clinton, South Carolina wished had never happened. On that day, Brian Adam Sanders was on the way to school when he lost control of his Ford Ranger truck and crashed head-on into an oncoming truck. He died on the way to the hospital, and the town of Clinton was shaken to its foundations.

Brian was a member of the Clinton High football team and a popular student on the school campus. His best friend and lifelong *brother*, Brandon Page, struggled over the next few months to come to terms with the tragedy of losing his best friend.

Flash forward eighteen months and Brandon was signing college scholarship papers for Presbyterian College. Sitting right next to him was his best friend's mom, Cindy Sanders, taking part in the ceremony at Clinton celebrating Brandon's college scholarship.

Brandon said, "I would like to say time has healed the wound, but it hasn't. A day doesn't go by that I don't think about him; each time I put on the cleats, I miss him. It is tough and still hard to believe he is not here."

Brandon and Brian had been friends since they were in daycare together a dozen years ago. As sixth graders, they started playing football together and became the best of friends over the years. Brandon was like a second son to the Sanders family—going with them on family campouts, fishing trips, and hunting trips.

But all that changed on September 10, 2002.

After the accident, Brandon remained close with Mrs. Sanders and the family, spending many nights at the Sanders' house as a way of coming to terms with Brian's death and helping to bring closure. Every time he dropped by, Mrs. Sanders was in the kitchen preparing his favorite foods and sharing his life experiences.

The 2003 season was Brandon's senior year at Clinton and would have been Brian's also. As the season started, Brian's mom was in her normal seat at the Red Devils home games. She cheered hard for the Devils. The Red Devils honored Brian that season by retiring his jersey number, forty-four. His spot on the field during warmups and drills was always held open, and his name was placed on the homecoming wall—a tradition recognizing senior football players at Clinton. It was not an easy season for the class of 2004 at Clinton but one in which they learned many of life's cruel lessons at an early age.

As the season ended, Brandon pursued his dream of college football. A trip to Presbyterian College left him knowing that PC was his new home, and he committed to the Blue Hose program.

On signing day 2004, as he fulfilled a lifelong dream of playing college football, the person sitting next to him and his parents was his best friend's mom, Mrs. Cindy Sanders.

Brandon said, "It would not have seemed right if she hadn't been there with us on such a special day. She saw me as her son, but I saw her as my second mom."

Brandon and Brian had always wanted to attend the same college. Events made that impossible, but Brandon feels Brian is also there and will feel his presence at Presbyterian College in the fall when he looks up in the stands and see his parents and Cindy Sanders cheering hard for the ex-Red Devil star

Clinton coach Andy Young credits Brandon for making a tragic situation a little more bearable for the Sanders family. He commented, "Brandon is a great young man who was part of our program for four years; it was tough for him losing his best friend. He befriended Brian's family and was there for them after the accident. He matured as a player and a young man. A school like ours never really gets over losing a young man like Brian. Even years from now, we will still feel his loss around here."

Coach Young also shared with us that Brian's parents supported and loved their son greatly. "They were here every day for every practice, come rain or shine. Even after the accident, they were still at the games and practices." In this case, Clinton Red Devil football helped the Sanders family deal with their unimaginable grief.

This spring as the senior moments and milestone commence, you can bet that Cindy Sanders will be there. She will have her camera out and will snap picture after picture when Brandon and his girlfriend, Catherine Cruickshanks, dress for the prom at Clinton. She will be a proud parent when Brandon walks across the stage in May and picks up his diploma. She was a proud parent last Wednesday when Brandon earned his college scholarship and signed his papers.

Next year, Brandon will study pre-law at Presbyterian College. On Saturdays, he will patrol the offensive line for the Blue Hose. Without a doubt, thoughts of Brian will be with him as moves into the next stage of his life. High school football in Clinton, South Carolina has certainly helped prepare him for college and for life. And in the face of tragedy, high school football provided a young man and a family with a moment of peace, if only briefly.

CHAPTER 20

Brandon's Admission Essay to Presbyterian College

Below is a copy of Brandon's essay, which he included on his application for admission to Presbyterian College. The message he sends here to all young people is important; it is even more powerful coming from someone who has lived through the events that Brandon has lived through.

Admission Essay to Presbyterian College
Brandon Page

On Tuesday, September 10, 2002, I lost a friend and a brother in a tragic car accident. Brian Adam Sanders was killed on the way to pick up his girlfriend, so they could go to school. But he never made it to her house.

He was driving down Barnes Road in Clinton, South Carolina, when he lost control of his 1999 Ford Ranger and was ejected from the vehicle after colliding head-on with an oncoming truck. He was not wearing his seatbelt and died that morning on the way to the hospital

That day, I lost a great friend who influenced my life greatly. Brian was like the brother I never had. He changed my perspective on life and the things I do every day.

Prior to Brian's death, I would get into my truck and drive somewhere as fast as I could—without wearing my seatbelt. But now, the first thing I do before driving away is put on my seatbelt. Since September tenth, I drive safely and cautiously.

I have also come to be thankful for all my friends because you never know how much they mean to you until they are gone. Brian has also impacted my life with his consistent "work hard, never quit" attitude. He was about five-feet, ten inches tall, weighed 160 pounds, and was a mean linebacker. He was not a big person, but he did not let that get in the way. He always worked ten times harder than anyone else did. If he got beaten at practice, he would only get beaten once because he never quit and was always ready to go again. He also helped me to see life from a different angle. He always lived life to the fullest and made everything he did enjoyable.

Since his death, he has brought me closer to the Lord. I have gotten back into church and realized that I am not invincible. I also realize now that an accident of the kind that took him could very well happen to me. Basically, Brian has saved my life. I have changed the way I do things, and I am attempting to live my life the best way possible. Brian has influenced my life tremendously, and I am grateful that I became good, close friends with him.

Brian always had a smile on his face and always thought of his friends first. Through his death, I have learned more about life and a great deal about friends and family. Brian was the one who brought me closer to all of the treasures of life. His friendship has made me a better person over the past year. I know his impact on my life will last forever. Brian not only influenced my life in these ways, but I see him as my guardian angel and my hero.

Brandon experienced some of the same things I went through as a young man by losing a friend. People can't tell you how they feel unless they personally go through a tragedy like we did when we were young. We never get over it. No, time does not heal. God does!

Things evolved for Brandon as the years went by; he changed his major to business and voluntarily ended his football career after his freshmen year at Presbyterian College. He wanted to concentrate on his studies, he told me later. It took Brandon a long time to be able to tell me that he was giving up football. He thought I would be disappointed in him. I told him that he was a grown man, and I would support whatever decision he made. I am very proud of both my children and their accomplishments. I am as proud a dad as a dad can be.

CHAPTER 21

You Don't Mess with Mama's Boy

As graduation was approaching for our son, it was a time for us to be happy as a family. Knowing that Brandon was finishing high school made us all proud. Brandon had been taking all honors classes and was looking forward to graduating.

Four weeks before graduation, the list of the top 20 percent of honor graduates was posted. Brandon's name wasn't on the list. How could that be? Brandon worked hard and had excellent grades; he deserved to be included. He only wanted what was rightfully his. With a GPA of 3.60, he should have been in the top 20 percent of those who made the list.

Brandon made several inquiries at the guidance office concerning his grades but was getting the run-around as usual. Kim made several calls to different people, but they didn't return her calls. Holding his head high, Brandon went on to graduate, knowing that the school system had failed him once again.

As parents, Kim and I weren't satisfied with what had happened. Brandon should have been acknowledged at graduation as an honor student, and he should have been able to wear the honor student banner. Kim made several calls after graduation, but she received no response. One of the guidance counselors called her back later and asked how she could fix the problem for the future. Kim and I went to the school's district office to look for some answers. We couldn't even get an appointment with the superintendent, nor could we get in to see the assistant superintendent. We continued to get the run-around. We finally decided to go see the principal at the high school.

The high school principal agreed to meet with us. During the meeting, I let Kim do most of the talking. I had become really upset at the way my son had been treated during football season and now this. During our discussion with the principal, I did raise the question as to why the names of the top 20 percent were posted four weeks before graduation. I asked him if the final exams actually mattered in deciding who made the list and who didn't. He agreed. During our discussion—and after reviewing Brandon's transcript—it appeared that omitting Brandon from the top 20 percent list was a mistake. Kim explained to the principal that the situation needed to be made right for Brandon—not us. Graduation was over, and the recognition that Brandon would have received for his achievements and hard work could never be replaced by a single apology. On behalf of the school, the principal wrote and sent a letter of recognition to Brandon.

It is our understanding that the way the school figures the top 20 percent of the class has been changed as a result of the mistake made with Brandon. I guess you can say that Brandon made a small contribution to the way things are now done at the local high school. (See school letter below.)

Clinton High School
A. Keith Bridges, Principal
North Adair Street
Clinton, SC 29325
Telephone 864-833-0817   FAX 864-833-0825

June 16, 2004

Brandon Page
177 Angler's Haven
Cross Hill, SC 29332

Dear Brandon:

I am writing to congratulate you on your designation as an Honor Graduate of the Class of 2004. After eighth semester grades were updated, your status changed to allow your designation for this distinction. I want to congratulate you on this accomplishment, the result of your diligence in your academic studies. We wish you much success in your future endeavors!

Sincerely,

A. Keith Bridges
Principal

CHAPTER 22

When I First Met Coach Bill Rhodes

Coach Bill Rhodes is still making his trips to the new high school at Clinton, as he has for over forty-five years. He is an icon at Clinton High and will be revered for many years to come. His stern voice has helped many students walk a straight line. Here is an extra chapter I wrote to Mr. Rhodes years ago entitled "When I Met Bill Rhodes." I have always been told the first encounter leaves a lasting impression. My first meeting with Coach Rhodes has remained important to my life for nearly forty-six years.

It was 1968 at Florida Street Junior High School, Clinton, South Carolina. I had just lost my dad to cancer on September the seventeen, during my first year of junior high school. With the heavy burden of my father's passing and having to enter a new school, I thought I was my own person. Little did I know that junior high had a dress code. Mr. John H. Fulmer summoned me to the principal's office over the loudspeaker during a math test in early October of the same year. On my way to the office— down those squeaky, crackling halls of Florida Street Junior High—I was wondering what I had done wrong. On arriving in Mr. Fulmer's office, he informed me that I was being sent home for not shaving my side burns—a violation of the student dress code.

And then it happened. Into the room walked a legend in his own time, the teacher and coach everyone labeled *Wild Bill*. Mr. Fulmer informed me that Coach Rhodes would drive me home and that I could return to school when I met the guidelines of the dress code. I was scared, but I did not let on that I was.

As we were driving to my house, I was surprised that Mr. Rhodes did not yell at or belittle me. He explained that there are a lot of things we must do in life we don't agree with: rules, guidelines, and of course dress codes. Having long side burns at that time was definitely against the rules. "Stay focused; this life is full of disappointments," he said. Mutual respect was given and observed during that ride.

Again, hardship hit my life. My brother was in a bad motorcycle accident, and I was kept out of school the rest of that year to help care for him. I went back to Florida Street for my second year in the seventh grade, which I passed. But during that year, Mr. Rhodes paddled me several times. Of course, I didn't do anything wrong, like throwing a football through a large old window, leaving study hall while Mr. Rhodes was talking to the Womecto drink machine man, or tossing out the window the green frog that sat on top of the intercom speaker in Mr. Rhodes's class.

Then it was time for my experience at Bell Street School. My father's last words to me were a request to finish school and have patience in all that I did. I am at about the 50 percent level of his wishes. I went on to finish Limestone College in Gaffney, South Carolina (3.894 GPA, magna cum laude), and to this day, I am working on having patience.

The days were somewhat different at Bell Street. Times were changing, the schools were being integrated, and Bell Street became an all-boys school. Some say that was the wrong decision, but looking back, I think it was the right one. I have often wondered why Mr. Rhodes was picked for a teacher and coach at Bell Street.

There were several small altercations between guys; one in particular involved a student named Bug. He started to bully folks around. Bug and I had one fight on the playground field during recess, and Mr. Rhodes and Mr. "Bulldog" Martin had to break it up. Mr. Rhodes took care of me then. He knew Bug and I had several classes together, so he made arrangements for me to be in his class (away from Bug) during the rest of that school year.

When the next year began, I had made up my mind to make good grades and get out of that mess. Well, Bug didn't forget, and there were several more altercations. Then it happened—*the big one*. Mr. Rhodes had to wrestle me to the ground as a huge brawl started, and about a dozen guys jumped me. Bug and a couple of others were expelled, and that year ended. But the conflict never left my mind. Occasionally, Mr. Rhodes and I still smile at each other, knowing we both remember that great ride I gave him as he rode me to the floor.

I had to help out at home and didn't have a chance to play sports until my junior year of high school. As I was struggling up the hill the first day of practice, I remember hearing a loud voice yelling, "You'll never make it a week, big boy; you'll quit before this week ends!"

That was a learning year for me because I had never played football except back-alley ball in the mill village. As I ran through what was known as the county fairgrounds, a loud voice would say, "Push harder; push harder." Of course, it was Coach Rhodes encouraging me. Clinton went on to have a good year. We finished the year thirteen to one.

I made up my mind that if I were going through the practices, I was going to start. My senior year, I started six football games, which was the highlight of my football days. Clinton went into the playoffs again that year, but I was sidelined with a head injury. We lost to James Island High School by two points; the final score was 17 to 15 in the state championship game. I remember that night as if it were only last night. After the game, Coach Rhodes came into the locker room and put his arm around me to let me know how proud he was of me that year. He is the only coach or person to ever say such words to me. That night, we grew loser as we shed tears of both victory and defeat. I recalled his words during that drive home from junior high, "Life is full of disappointments, but you have to keep your head up."

Well, I went on to graduate from high school but was again dealt a blow. I was in a bad car wreck behind Presbyterian College on August 31, 1975. I lost two friends and blamed myself for the wreck. The first person at my side that night was Coach Rhodes. As I was struggling for life, he and I shared information that only he and I can recall, and it is better left between us. I want to think him for his compassion and understanding.

Our paths still cross from time to time. One recent encounter was at the 2001 spring athletic banquet at Clinton High School. When Coach Rhodes stood and spoke about all his students, tears flowed from every eye in the gymnasium. I was proud to be one of the hundreds of sons he helped raise. I recalled a lot of good times we had through the years and the positive influence he exerted over me. I want to thank him for his confidence in me, even as I continue to struggle about the accident twenty-six years ago. I learned a lot from Coach Rhodes in the classroom and on the playing field, but most of all I learned a lot about life.

If my playing ability had equaled the respect I have for this man, I would have been all-conference in football. But in the game of life, I am an *all-American* for knowing him!

Thanks, coach; may God continue to bless you and your family.

—Ronny "Roundman" Page

CHAPTER 23

*A Tribute to my Friend,
Gene "Big Gene" Pinson*

While preparing this book, my good friend and business partner, Gene Pinson, passed away in January 2010. Gene was the type of guy who would ask you how you were doing even when he was in pain himself. I never heard Gene complain. He would call and check on me at least once a week, if not more frequently. Gene and I both were good-sized fellows, but Gene's heart was bigger than life. He would've given you the shirt off his back if you needed it.

I think Gene really found his calling in life being on the radio each morning. He loved WLBG in Laurens, South Carolina, and the talk show he and Randy Stevens broadcast each morning. I always told folks that the call letters *WLBG* stood for "We Love Big Gene." Many in the Laurens and Clinton areas will truly miss Gene. So many stories, so many good times we had over those years. Often, while making burgers at Red's Burger Masters, he would carry on a conversation with people and never miss a beat. Many folks loved to come in to the restaurant just to say hello to Gene.

Gene loved his family and did everything he could for them. He always put himself last. Gene is now looking down on all of us with a smile. He and Marvin, his father-in-law, are watching their beloved dirt track racing from the best box seats anyone could have. Love and miss you, big guy!

Big Gene on the air for WLBG photo by Randy Stevens

Gene and I both took pride in the operations of Red's Burger Masters. We felt that we had a small but positive influence on the lives of the guys we hired. We felt that we contributed to each one's outlook on life. We gave these guys jobs to help keep them busy and to teach them about life. Gene was always a young man at heart. I would like to share a letter Paul Finley emailed to me after I contacted him about Gene's passing. It brought tears to my eyes.

January 18, 2010

Ron,

Thank you for letting me know of Gene's passing Saturday night. I actually got the news before I went to bed, and I couldn't sleep a wink, thinking about Gene. I haven't seen Gene in a long time, but we shared a few emails over the past few years.

Time fades some of the memories I have of working with you and Gene so many years ago. However, time will never fade the love I have for both of you. I hope Gene knew what a positive figure he was in my life during my teenage years. I'm not sure I ever really said it to him, but I hope he understood the unspoken feeling. Therefore, I'm telling the same to you now. I want you to know how fortunate I feel about working with you both at such a young age. You and Gene were like extra fathers to me, and I am grateful I was able to grow personally as a result. The lessons I learned in those years were invaluable, and I am a better person, husband, and father as a result.

I used to take heat at times from classmates and friends about working at Red's Burger Masters. Some poked fun of me because I was working (while others were out wasting time) or because I smelled like a hamburger after work or because I was seen driving Gene's old black van around town. However, what none of them understood was that it was more than a job. It was a place of fun, pride, and life lessons. My years at Red's Burger Masters taught me the value of hard work, friendship, trust, and capital. I met so many people in college who were ill-prepared for college and independent life in general. They didn't have what I had growing up, and all this new responsibility came crashing down hard. I learned a lot about those things early on at Red's, and the experience was a blessing.

I remember a lot of goofing off while we were working; on the surface, it seemed like we were all a bunch of kids to an outsider. However, there was no mistaking that the fun only lasted as long as hard work and genuine effort followed. We all knew that when Ron turned into business mode play time was over!

To say I will miss Gene is wrong. I've been missing Gene for many years. However, I am greatly saddened at the fact that such a good friend has passed, and I didn't get to say goodbye or tell him all the things I wanted him to hear. I'm confident that he has had the same impact on others that he had on me. He was one of a kind, and his memory and spirit will live on for many years to come.

I am taking tomorrow off and driving in from Atlanta to pay my respects. At this point, it is all I can do for my friend Gene.

—Paul

CHAPTER 24

Another Touch of God's Hand

After I had to retire, I started seeing a local doctor in Clinton as my primary care doctor. He would do regular checks on my bloodwork and keep me informed about the results. During a routine visit in 2007, he ordered an echocardiogram of my heart. On a follow-up visit, he went over the results of my test. I noticed that the results were faxed to the doctor's office on October 31, 2007. (Remember this month and day.)

My doctor informed me I had an enlarged heart and a heart valve that was not functioning as it should. He ordered for me the necessary medicines to start taking. I visited my primary doctor about every three months afterward. During one follow-up visit in April 2012, I noticed that my doctor was checking my pulse and heart rates more closely than he had done during previous visits. After listening for a while, he informed me that he wanted me to go straight to the emergency room to be admitted to the hospital. My heart was in atrial fibrillation and my heart rate was 157 beats per minute. I informed him that I would go home first and then to the ER.

As I arrived home, my brother was pulling up. I explained to Kim what was happening and asked her to get my things together.

My brother said he would drop me off at the emergency room. After being admitted, Kim arrived; I filled her in on the fact that I was scheduled to have a cardioversion procedure the next morning. Knowing that Kim had an important doctor's visit in Spartanburg the next morning, I sent her home so that she could rest and make it to her appointment. I could tell she didn't want to leave, but I told her I would be okay and that I would call her early in the morning to get her up.

The next morning, as promised, I began calling home. I made about twenty calls, to no avail. I grew uneasy, so I called my son, Brandon, and my daughter, Michelle. Brandon said that he would head to our house to see what was going on. Brandon called me back and said that his mom's car was at the house, but there was no sign of her. Michelle had also arrived at our house. I called Brandon back and told him to rewind the surveillance system to see if he could see anything. I hung up the phone and called for the nurse. I began to take out my IVs myself. I informed the nurse I was leaving because I had an emergency at home. The nurse told me that I was five minutes away from the procedure to correct my heart. I advised the nurse, "I am not going to be put to sleep until I know my wife is okay!"

After looking at the security system, Brandon could tell that the neighbors had visited, and Kim had left with them. Michelle went over to their house, and sure enough, Kim was there. She had gotten sick and went to stay with them. They said it was too late to call anyone. Kim said that they were going to call early that morning, but they had overslept. The neighbors apologized.

Meantime, I was being discharged. The nurse was worried that I would have a heart attack or stroke if I left the hospital without the procedure. As soon as I got the medicine the doctor ordered, I was headed home. Arriving home and seeing that Kim was alright, I was at ease.

Kim didn't get any better and was admitted into Spartanburg Regional on August twentieth. She had a twenty-six-day stay and was discharged on September fourteenth. After she got home and felt better, I decided to reschedule my heart procedure. I was still in atrial fibrillation, and my heart rate was still at 157 beats per minute. I had the cardioversion done on October thirty-first. Remember the month and day on the fax that was sent to my primary care doctor about my bad heart valve and enlarged heart? It was the same month and day.

Waking up after the procedure, the doctor asked me how I was doing. I said that I felt fine. He said the procedure went well and that my rhythms and rates were in the normal ranges. Prior to the procedure, my neighbor, Leon Easler, had made the trip to be there because the doctor was going to stop my heart and restart it. I asked Leon to say a prayer before I was put to sleep. Kim, Michelle, and Leon stepped out into the hall. They said they heard me flatline on the monitor and then heard a thumping sound. After leaving the hospital, I told everyone that something good had happened, which was more than just repairing the heart rate and rhythm problems.

I had a follow-up visit two weeks later with the cardiologist. During my visit, the doctor informed me that everything was in rhythm and sounded good. Then I asked him what we were going to do about my enlarged heart and bad valve, which had showed up on the test. He looked puzzled. He stepped out of the room for about five minutes and came back in. He said, "Mr. Page, you don't have an enlarged heart or bad valve."

I shouted, "Hallelujah!"

That's enough to give anyone glory bumps. A third touch from God! None of my doctors could explain to me in medical terms what had happened on the operating table that day, but I know a man who can. His name is Jesus!

CHAPTER 25

The Reason I Wrote My Story

I wasn't looking for pity in writing about my life's experiences. I know that others have been through worse situations than I have. I have no ill feelings toward anyone because I am not the man I used to be. I have forgiven everyone!

I write about my life's experiences hoping that, through God, they will help someone understand that no matter what you are facing, there is someone who can help you. His name is Jesus Christ. No matter how wide the river is you are trying to cross, no matter how deep the valley is you are going through, or no matter how high the mountain is you are climbing, there is help. Whatever your situation is God can help you through it!

As a young man and as an adult, I have experienced many situations that deeply, emotionally impacted my entire life. God only knows why or how I have endured them all. I am confident that he has a plan for my life and that he has helped me through all the experiences I have faced.

It only takes a few seconds to have your world turned upside down, as mine was on August 31, 1975. God shed his grace on me several times for some reason, and I pray I haven't missed the reason. There is so much for which I am grateful. I have experienced many miracles since the night of that wreck. God healed my life after three doctors called the family to my bedside.

The first miracle is my understanding wife, Kim. She has stood beside me and supported me in ways no other person has. The other miracles are my daughter, Michelle, my son, Brandon, and my granddaughters, Dakota, Whitney, and Riley, whom all I love so dearly. For if God had chosen to take me the night of that wreck, none of them would be here today. As I look back at all the stress and life situations I've endured, God is the only one who could have helped me through them.

I wish for everyone an endless supply of blessings the Bible calls the fruits of the Spirit. If we've never thought of ourselves as rich, we simply need to read the first half of Ephesians, and it will open our eyes to everything God has given us. The Bible provides us with excellent information on this topic. It describes a city whose builder and maker is God. This is a huge, well-illuminated, joyful city; it is set aside from violence, sickness, sin, and death. We all need to claim and count his blessings. What the Lord has done for each of us will surprise us all. It certainly has me—my salvation!

Salvation is the most important thing in the world, both now and in the hereafter. If you are not saved, nothing else matters. If you are reading this and you don't know the Lord, please take time to know him. If you have been putting off being saved or think that you may one day choose salvation, let today be that day. You may not get another chance like I did. Even if you are lukewarm in your belief, it's time to start over. The Spirit of God said through John,

> I know your works, that you are neither cold nor hot. I could wish you were cold or hot. So, then, because you are lukewarm, and neither cold nor hot, I will vomit you out of My mouth. Because you say, "I am rich, have

become wealthy, and have need of nothing'-and do not know that you are wretched, miserable, poor, blind, and naked- I counsel you to but from Me gold refined in the fire, that you may be rich; and white garments, that you may be clothed, that the shame of your nakedness may not be revealed; and anoint your eyes with eye salve, that you may see. As many as I love, I rebuke and chasten. Therefore be zealous and repent. Behold, I stand at the door and knock. If anyone hears My voice and opens the door, I will come in to him and dine with him, and he with Me. (Revelation 3:15–20 KJV)

It is time for us to wake up and get on fire for God! Regardless of your past, today is your day to rise above all of the hits you have taken and start over.

Becoming a believer does not exempt you from problems, but I testify it will help you through each one of them. You will continue to make mistakes, but as a believer in Christ, you have a way to ask him to forgive you. His grace is *free!* Asking Jesus into your heart is very simple. Read the following. If you agree with your heart, you are saved. Pick up a Bible and begin reading the New Testament. Don't be ashamed of the Lord! From time to time, you may stumble and fall, but Jesus will be there to pick you up. If you fill in your heart that you want to be saved, repeat this simple prayer.

> Dear God,
>
> I know I am a sinner and that I owe the sin debt. I also believe that Jesus Christ was born of a virgin, died on the cross in my place, and rose from the dead. His death paid in full what I owe as a sinner. Here and now I trust him as my Savior. From this moment on, I am fully depending on him for my salvation. Amen!

Red's and Red's Burger Masters
World-Famous Chili

As promised, below is the secret recipe of Red's and Red's Burger Masters chili, which is over eighty years old. Gene Pinson and Ronny Page were the last two to know the entire secret and process. If you have any problems, you can email Ronny Page for help at ronepage68@aol.com.

[This recipe uses two pounds of hamburger meat.]

1. Mix meat and water by hand to the consistency of oatmeal; use enough water to cover the meat well. Note: water should cook down.
2. Cook meat for two hours on medium heat, stirring so as not to stick or scorch the meat when it comes to a boil. Note: add more water if needed.
3. Add 5 1/2 tablespoons of a name-brand chili powder. Add more if a stronger taste is desired; my preference is Sauers. Add 3 tablespoons of salt or salt to taste.
4. Add 3 tablespoons of real butter. This is a must!
5. Add 3 tablespoons of a name-brand black pepper, or pepper to taste. The more you use the hotter it will be, preferably Sauers.
6. Add 1 tablespoon of cayenne pepper, preferably Sauers.
7. Key: add 4 saccharin tablets. (No, it's not enough to hurt anyone.)
8. Add 1/2 to 3/4 cup of ketchup.

A key factor is to add all seasonings after the meat is done; let it cook on the lowest heat for about forty-five minutes to one hour. Enjoy!

The Big Red Spicy Hamburger
"The Big Red"

1. 6 ounces of hamburger meat
2. 1 tablespoon of garlic salt
3. 1 tablespoon of Tabasco sauce
4. 1 teaspoon of salt
5. 1 tablespoon of Worcestershire sauce
6. Tony's Cacciatore cajun seasoning (any Cajun spice will work)
7. 1 tablespoon of catsup
8. Mix well into a patty and cook slowly.

Note: This was a creation of Red Pinson's wife, Mrs. Toni Pinson, in the early 1960s.

In memory of family members and friends who have gone to be with the Lord:

James Richard "Jim" Page Sr. (my father)
Wayne Power (my father-in-law)
Mike Johnson
Joe Cothran
Alan "Ears" Petty
David Campbell
Jacob Hill
Jamie Ray King
Brian Sanders
Gene "Big Gene" Pinson
Tim Mann
Mitchell Moore
Smilie Martin
Walt Evans
Louie Webb
Butch Brewington

Printed in the United States
By Bookmasters